Big Kiss

"Makes me wish I knew more struggling actors."

—Daniel Handler, *Newsday*

"I'd like to thank the Academy and all of the little people who made Henry Alford's hilarious book possible. Mr. Alford delivers a performance that is laugh-out-loud funny and written with high style."

—Christopher Buckley, author of *Little Green Men*

"A delightful narrative . . . Rendering his vignettes with a clever mix of description and drollery, Alford displays a gift for scene . . . When Alford finally succeeds, readers will rejoice that he's found his well-deserved place 'in the glamour trenches' at last."

—*Publishers Weekly* (starred review)

"A witty, delightful memoir . . . Alford relates his adventures with marvelous tartness . . . but [he] is funniest describing a kinda spoiled, kinda talented suburban boy, lost in the wilds of London, L.A. and New York—himself."

—*Booklist*

"Henry Alford has more sparkle than a diamond store . . . [*Big Kiss*] is cheeky and smart, but good-natured, and, unlike the work of a lot of contemporary humorists, generous."

—*Las Vegas Weekly*

"Hilarious . . . Alford combines his journalistic eye for detail with his Wildean sense of the ridiculous . . . [H]is gleefully sardonic style produces innumerable full-on, spill-your-drink kind of laughs . . . some of the funniest writing around."

—*Fort Lauderdale City Link*

"[Alford's] wit and hilarious exactitude proves he is a hit man of humor."

—*Columbus Alive*

Thunderous Applause for Henry Alford

"A classicist, firmly in the mold of Wilde, Waugh, Benchley, and Lebowitz . . . humor that demands to be savored on the printed page."
—*The New York Times Book Review*

"Writing in the mode of S. J. Perelman and Flann O'Brien, Alford produces pieces of participatory journalism that are arch, smart, and exquisitely absurd." —*The Village Voice Literary Supplement*

"New York prankster? Manhattan Monkeyshine Maven? . . . I haven't decided what to call Henry Alford . . . Clinical-Trial Comedian? . . . Freelance Funster? . . . I think I've got it: Very funny writer."
—*Newsday*

"Henry Alford is the postmodern George Plimpton . . . he is also a talented and terrifically funny writer."
—David Owen, author of *The Walls Around Us*

"I haven't had this much fun reading since I found Fran Lebowitz."
—Lorenzo Music, creator of *The Bob Newhart Show*
(and voice of Carlton the Doorman)

"Alford's strong point is a sort of manic ever-willingness to go do something, even if—especially if—the task requires ritual self-humiliation." —*The Washington Post Book World*

"Hip and urban, but without smugness or cruelty . . . Alford adopts an innocent, earnest pose when venturing into these strange new worlds, and his writing is crisp and funny." —*The Boston Book Review*

Big Kiss

ALSO BY HENRY ALFORD

Out There

Municipal Bondage

HENRY ALFORD

Big Kiss

One Actor's
Desperate Attempt
to Claw His Way
to the Middle

Broadway Books
New York

A portion of the chapter on wearing pajamas originally appeared in *The New York Times Magazine,* and a portion of the chapter on perfume spraying originally appeared in *Vogue.*

Broadway Books titles may be purchased for business or promotional use or for special sales. For information, please write to: Special Markets Department, Random House, Inc., 1540 Broadway, New York, NY 10036.

First Broadway Books trade paperback edition published 2001.

Designed by Barbara M. Bachman

Library of Congress Cataloging-in-Publication Data
Alford, Henry, 1962–
Big kiss: one actor's desperate attempt to claw his way to the middle/Henry Alford.
p.   cm.
Originally published: New York: Villard, c2000.
1. Alford, Henry, 1962–   2. Actors—United States—Biography.   I. Title.
PN2287 .A47 A3 2001
792'.028'092—dc21
[B]
2001025203

ISBN 0-7679-0741-8

1   3   5   7   9   10   8   6   4   2

For Sandra Loh

Prologue

I SHUDDER TO THINK. By what processes is the soul perverted? One day I was an affable if misguided beginner—not unlike the foreigner who has learned English by audiotape and who now greets all passersby, "Lesson One. Good morning!"—and the next I was a bitter striver, desperate for recognition.

Rejected by directors, ignored by casting people, unable to set in motion that chain of events that would lead to gainful employment as a performer, I had decided to vault over the wearisome, shoe-leather part of the job—the part where you actually perform—and instead proceed directly to fame: I would convince various New York City delicatessens, dry cleaners, and restaurants to hang my eight-by-ten on their walls.

"If you hang up my picture," I told one waitress in desperation, "I'll tell ten friends about your restaurant."

"Sort of a trade, like," she responded, wiping the counter, deftly wrangling a piece of lettuce whose curlicued edge suggested labial frill.

"Very much a trade," I said.

Scowling slightly, she asked, "How would I know which ones are your friends?"

I thought aloud, "Maybe they could talk in code."

"Okay," she said, brightening. "Like how, though?"

"When asked for their order, each could request to speak to Fat Man and Little Boy."

She looked at me as if I were undermedicated. "I don't think so, hon."

....

MY FIRST VISIT had been to a brightly lit delicatessen just east of Times Square on Forty-third Street. Clutching a manila envelope that contained twenty of my head shots, I asked the gentleman behind the register, "Do you put performers' head shots up?"

"No."

"Do you want to start to?"

"No."

Message received. Please go away.

At Metro Deli, on Eighth Avenue at Forty-eighth, home of the "Delicatessen Hall of Fame"—a wall featuring the smiley visages of Elizabeth Taylor, Willard Scott, and Paul Sorvino, as well as several nonfamous individuals—I asked a manager how the nonfamous individuals had gotten up on the wall. He said, "Some are friends, or people who've eaten here."

"Well," I said, pointing to my half-empty soup bowl, "I've eaten here."

"Yes."

"So, could I . . ."

He took my eight-by-ten from me. I explained that I was a humorist who had been a guest on several notable talk shows, and that I was trying to do more performing.

"So, you . . . act?" he asked.

"I've done a lot of really good scene work," I assured him. He appeared unmoved. I added, "But I have very prominent eyebrows, so I'm thinking I could get cast as someone who just invented something."

A pressing, silverware-related matter suddenly occupied him, and he flitted off, my picture in hand.

But had he taken the picture just to get rid of me? I would later find out that indeed he had. I was similarly indulged by fourteen other establishments, including the restaurant where I had suggested that my friends could speak in code, and the Carnegie Deli, where I had tried to convince the harried manager, "I think it's a face we like. It's not a face we *know,* but it's a face we like."

ONE OF THE first places to hang me up was Ms. Buffy's French Cleaners. A small, friendly dry cleaning concern on Eighth Avenue between Fifty-third and Fifty-fourth, Ms. Buffy's showcases, over its main counter, framed pictures of both musicians (the Village People and the Ink Spots, among others) and actors (Jerry Orbach and Obba Babatundé, among others). I asked the kindly young man behind the counter if newcomers were ever included in the collection; he told me, "Sometimes."

"Because some of these people are dead," I pointed out. "Some are recently dead, but others are, unh, really quite dead."

"Most of these people are still coming in," he told me.

I didn't want to quibble. In the same way that emperors and statesmen of the classical world were, when immortalized on temples, depicted as youths in their peak physical condition, so, too, do modern entertainers radiate, in head-shot collections, a false vigor. I pressed my cause; the man told me to ask his boss. Seconds later the boss materialized and reported, "I don't have any more frames."

I suggested I might bring one in.

"Yes, maybe," he said noncommittally. The employee I'd been speaking with added, "Try to get black so it fits in with the other ones."

Adjacent to Ms. Buffy's is a pharmacy where, for $2.69, I

bought a black frame. I presented the Ms. Buffy's boss with my head shot in its new frame. He smiled, shaking his head in slight disbelief.

"Yes. Looks good," he said. "I'll put a nail in."

I also had luck at Park West Valet Cleaners on West Fifty-seventh Street. When I had plunked down my eight-by-ten on the counter, a female employee in her forties asked me, "Will you sign it?" I readily assented and, in fact, had brought along a black Magic Marker for just such purposes. Once I had signed it, the woman twirled the eight-by-ten so she could see my signature. But she did not pick the picture up; so, sensing a lack of full-bore enthusiasm, I suggested, "I could write 'Love ya!' or 'Big kiss' on it, too."

"Then it will look like we know each other."

"Yes," I said, "it would connote warmth."

I opted for "Love ya!," thanked the woman heartily, and left. Shortly thereafter, walking down Seventh Avenue, I found myself gazing at the prominent placement of Dustin Hoffman's and Tony Danza's head shots in the window of Piermont Cleaners between Fifty-fourth and Fifty-fifth. I started to approach the establishment's door but then thought, No, no—I already have good dry cleaner exposure.

But dining establishments remained a more elusive target. One restaurant owner told me that some members of his profession will buy famous people's head shots at memorabilia stores and then hang them up, like cavemen painting on their walls the meat sources they hope to slaughter. But I was having trouble even *giving* my head shot away.

Denied, I became envious. One day, after enjoying a delicious piece of lasagna at Vincent's in Little Italy, I started talking to my waiter.

"She's wonderful," I said, pointing to Ann Jillian's head shot on the wall; the picture is inscribed, "So-o good every time we come to visit! And we love what you did with the new look. Ann Jillian."

"But I was eating over at Taormina the other night?" I continued. "She signed her picture over there, 'Taormina Restaurant is my home in Little Italy. There is no finer food.' "

The waiter's expression betrayed a small amount of confusion. Pulling one of my own head shots out from a manila envelope, I said, "With this picture, however, I would be willing to go exclusive."

The waiter blinked at the floor, not anxious to be saddled with a new duty. He told me to give it to the manager; I did, but to no avail.

Several blocks away, at another restaurant, I tried a new tack. "You have such amazing people," I told my waiter. "I can't even imagine being included in their ranks."

Neither, apparently, could he. So, pointing to a picture of the *Mothers-in-Law* costar Kaye Ballard and her three poodles—"Pinky, Pockets, and Big Shirl Ballard"—signed, "We *all* love your pasta! Amoré, Katherina," I claimed that I was friends with the Ballards. The waiter looked not unimpressed.

"I love that Pockets," I added. "That Ragú spot he did? Some of his best work, his very best."

The waiter did not take my bait. So I continued, "But I think there's a little competitiveness between him and Big Shirl." Pausing in an effort to suggest the onset of insider information, I reported, "Pockets is sort of the Ballard family's Eve Harrington."

The waiter's gaze shifted to my water glass, which he promptly filled.

I FINALLY HAD a breakthrough. When the warm, mustachioed proprietor of the Star Diner on the corner of Fifty-fourth and Seventh told me, "I don't have much space," I reached into my manila envelope and pulled Dustin Hoffman's autographed eight-by-ten ("To Henry. Peace, Dustin Hoffman") which I had collected as a teenager.

"I also have a Dustin Hoffman if that would, unh, grease the wheel," I said. The proprietor registered no emotion.

"Or, look," I continued, reaching once more into the envelope. "Telly."

A three-by-five of a late-career Telly Savalas ("To Henry. Your beautiful baby, Telly Savalas").

"Oh, yes," the proprietor said, visibly warming.

"That's a nice one," I responded. "A lot of restaurant people like that one. He's fat *and* he's famous—that sends a good message to your diners."

"Yes, I like this one quite a lot. It's small, too, so it would fit."

"Great. But you understand: if you take Telly, you take Henry."

The twinkle in his eye went slightly milky.

I pointed out, "We're a package."

"Okay," he said. He sighed, and in that sigh I detected a sea change: the world was finally capitulating to my strivings. "I'll do it."

Armed with my Dustin Hoffman, as well as with pictures of Bette Midler, Betty Ford, and Kim Novak, among others, I pressed on, striking gold at three delis, one restaurant, and one more dry cleaner.

⸻

EARLY THAT EVENING I hied myself to the Carnegie Deli again, where my picture had not been hung up but where I had decided to partake of some pastrami anyway. I fell into conversation with two nearby diners—a middle-aged couple from

New Jersey. I explained to them that I was a writer who was trying to do more performing but that I was having trouble finding my niche.

"You know how Olympia Dukakis has settled nicely into Grandmother with Pottymouth, or how Jeff Goldblum is sort of Mr. Insectoid Genius?" I asked.

"Yes," the wife said uncertainly, sipping her soup.

"I'm looking for that. Or maybe it's not even acting per se, maybe it's just some performance-related thing."

"What do you mean?" the wife asked.

"Well, like our waiter. He always has a funny line when people come in. He's found his thing. Or like Michael Moore, the guy who made that documentary *Roger and Me*. He's found his place."

The husband, picking up his sandwich, proposed, "It's like you want to provide a service."

I thought about this. "Yes."

"Okay."

I looked over at the wall, at the many entertainers and actors and other personalities; then I looked across the room, where our waiter was making a customer grin. Each, it seemed, had found his niche.

I wondered, Will I find mine?

One

"AT THE END OF the four weeks, you'll know whether or not you should continue acting."

On the first day of the summer session of the Royal Academy of Dramatic Art, these slightly ominous words tumbled from the mouth of Peter Craze, the ruggedly handsome director overseeing the division of fourteen actors in which RADA had placed me. I was sitting with my colleagues in a vast, white classroom on the third floor of RADA's annex, where, as I gazed out the sunshine-drenched windows overlooking Chenies Street in the Bloomsbury area of London, I had started to daydream. I had been thinking about notable RADA graduates who had performed Hamlet—John Gielgud, Kenneth Branagh, and Ralph Fiennes came to mind—which, in a tiny flare-up of ego, had led me to wonder if *I* would ever get to tackle the Dane. Suddenly I saw myself backstage at a venerable West End theater, nervously pacing on my opening night. Beside me is RADA's patron, the Queen, who, earlier in her chambers has fed my anxiety about playing Hamlet by exhorting me to "do it for RADA, old boy!" I peer out into the audience from the wings, and my eyes bulge with amazement: the theater is so vast! Will I ever be able to fill it with golden sound? Her

Majesty lays her hand on my shoulder and then counsels, "Breath support, dearie!"

························

BUT, SOFT, WHAT'S THIS? *Whether or not you should continue acting* . . . A note of potential doom. An asp in the proverbial garden, a rodent in my very leotard. Casting a glance at my fellow actors, I grew concerned: had I flown all the way to London, my copy of Shakespeare's collected works clutched to my bosom, only to learn that money-making and tights-wearing were, as far as I was concerned, mutually exclusive concepts? Had I ponied up close to three thousand dollars for training and accommodations and meals, only to be told to keep my day job? Granted, we summer-session students had not, like the students in the three-year program, had to audition, and so there were likely to be some stargazers whose illusions would be shattered. But was I to be one of them? Craze—an actor and director with West End and off-Broadway credits—explained that on the last day of the monthlong session, he would meet with each one of us privately and deliver his sentence.

An image popped into my mind: A Heathrow customs official presses a handheld stamp into an inkpad and then emblazons my forehead CARGO.

························

I HAD FALLEN asleep at the banquet of Life; at some point during my thirty-fourth year, the better part of my spirit and personality seemed to have crawled under the covers. I had become reclusive and slightly sullen; I showed little or no interest in working with others or in making new friends. My six-year relationship with my boyfriend, Jess, too, was showing signs of stasis.

Where was my zest? Where was my verve? I was rapidly becoming the mope of Greenwich Village.

At about the same time that I became aware of my gradual brownout, I had an epiphany. Namely, that three of the peak moments of my adult life had hinged on, or involved, performing. A magazine article I wrote in 1991 had landed me on *The Tonight Show*. A reading I had given in New York City had led to my first book deal. And I had decided that Jess was the man for me when, on our second date, he agreed to my suggestion that we read each other our favorite short stories.

Like you, I was in *Oklahoma!* in high school; I wore a series of colorful bandanas and uttered one line, "Don't tetch 'im— he's daid," stretching out *daid* to at least two syllables. In nursery school in New Haven, asked what farm animal I wanted to be in the class play, I had opted for "earthworm." In short, I had not been without early signs of professional aptitude.

But once I became an adult, I formed that essentially elitist opinion that most people have toward actors: if actors are successful, we can be drawn to them with near-religious intensity, subtly altering our opinions and habits as a result of our infatuation; if they are unsuccessful, we view them as deluded self-promoters who are prone to wearing rainbow suspenders and to nattering or about "mask work."

These feelings were exacerbated when, just after college, I worked for four years in the film industry, as an associate to a casting director named Joy Todd. Brought into almost daily contact with professional performers, I came to think of the truly talented ones as beautiful musical instruments, capable of producing almost any sound; the untalented or unschooled ones seemed like strangely large kazoos, best relegated to long-term storage.

My story is not wholly emblematic: as someone who writes for a number of national magazines, I have something that most struggling performers do not. Indeed, almost all of the professional engagements that I have secured as a performer have had something to do with the fact that I am a writer. While

I would never suggest to prospective employers that my engagement might bring them or their projects one step closer to that bitch goddess, Publicity, nor would I take steps toward this unethical end, I am never privy to the decisions that surround my hiring. It is said that Jerry Lewis used to "forget" his briefcase in the offices wherein he had met with directors, producers, and casting people; the suspicion was that, once the briefcase was retrieved, Lewis could play back a tape in a tape recorder therein. My sense of decorum and my fear of physical violence would prohibit this.

I did not set out to become either of the Toms, Cruise or Hanks. Nor did I think that I would be transformed from a fairly emotionally restrained individual into a gushing fountain. Rather, I wanted to find some kind of performing that I enjoyed doing and was good at, in the hope that it might spur me on to reengage with life.

And then, one day, it might happen: a starstruck fan might indulgently ask, "And did someone tell me you do a little *writing* as well?"

AT AN INITIATION meeting for us eighty RADA summer students, Ellis Peters, the ruddy, eggplant-shaped director of the summer program, told us, "You'll be working your socks off." He also pleaded, "Please don't put 'trained at RADA' on your CV's and résumés. We reserve that for the three-year students." This second comment inspired looks of disappointment on a few faces; what good was buying a little prestige if you weren't allowed to flaunt it?

We recited; we memorized; we seized any opportunity to utter the phrase "with a bare bodkin." Classes met from nine to five Monday through Friday; in addition to the three hours a day that each of the five divisions would spend with their director rehearsing a play or a series of scenes to be presented on the last day of classes, each division would also have an hour of voice and an hour of movement a day. Other classes included stage fighting, speech, tumbling, Elizabethan dance, and seminars on Elizabethan history.

We tromped from classroom to classroom, from the John Gielgud Studio to the Charles Laughton Room ("Excuse me," one of my classmates said to me one day, "I'm looking for the Gary Oldman Toilet.")

My group was a cosmopolitan one—of the fourteen actors, six of us hailed from the States, two from England, two from Belgium, and one each from Denmark, Canada, Japan, and Italy; the average age was twenty-seven, and most had at least a little experience performing Shakespeare. And so we formed a tiny United Nations of thespian ardor; together we endeavored to lengthen our spines and to relax our lower jaws and to transform the pedestrian "I grant the duke" into a pear-shaped "I grahnt the dewque." Fortunately, there were limits to our ardor—when our speech teacher announced in our first class with her, "Henry has tension in his upper lip, and I want you all to remind him of it as often as possible," my colleagues, bless them, did not comply.

In one early exercise, we took turns reading a scene between Kent and Oswald in *King Lear*. Cast as Kent, I got to call my scene partner first a "knave; a rascal; an eater of broken meats; a base, proud, shallow, beggarly, three-suited, hundred-pound filthy worsted-stocking knave; a lily-liver'd, action-taking . . . , whoreson, glass-gazing, super-serviceable, finical rogue; one-trunk-inheriting slave," and next "a son and heir of a mongrel bitch," and, finally, a "whoreson cullionly barber-monger." I based my character interpretation on a prominent New York City divorce attorney.

MY FAVORITE CLASS was tumbling. In our first session, our small, wiry instructor, Terry, explained that we would start by learning how actors pull hair, choke, bite, stomp on someone's foot, and scratch; I whispered to Donald, the happy-go-lucky Dane in my group, "I can't wait to get cast in the next Bette Davis picture." Terry would look at one of us, say, "Can I have a borrow of you?" and then use that person as a demonstration model/stunt puppet. After he had taught us the five moves, he encouraged us to pair up and string together three or more of these moves in a sequence. I paired up with Tracey, a twenty-eight-year-old with swimsuit modeling and a *Baywatch* appearance in her past.

I suggested, "How about you're tying your sneaker, and I come up and scream, 'That's my sneaker!' and then bite you."

Tracey, one of the sunnier individuals I have ever met, betrayed a small amount of discomfort with my proposal. "I don't know . . ."

"We don't have to," I started to back down.

"No, no, it sounds okay. Just, umm, just show me how we would do it."

We worked out a brief scene—Tracey, on bent knee, was tying her sneaker. I approached from stage left, screamed, "You bitch, that's my sneaker!" and bit her left arm. She rose on the bite and wriggled free; I spat out the arm nugget; she choked me violently till I collapsed on the floor, apparently dead. But as she walked away, I reanimated, grabbed a hank of her hair, twirled her 360 degrees, and banged her head on the floor, inducing unconsciousness. I removed her sneakers and walked away. But then Tracey revived and shot me dead.

We ran through it twice, Tracey adding wonderful embellishments in the form of grunting; her strangling technique was equally solid. Finding ourselves with a minute or two of free time, we watched classmates Anna and Dorothy rehearse their routine; when the tiny Anna fell to the ground in her death throes, her left leg convulsed in a highly unconvincing manner that was equal parts Folies Bergère and dwarf bowling.

"Very showy," I sniffed to Tracey.

"Yes," she agreed.

"But we have *narrative*."

PERFORMING SHAKESPEARE, AS they say, is exhausting—only royalty ever get to sit. Chief among Craze's ambitions for our dramatic education was to have us perform Shakespeare as the Elizabethans had. He was adamant about using the First Folio, the 1623 edition of the plays, probably based on Shakespeare's manuscripts or promptbooks that were still in the possession of his acting company; in the First Folio, *bosom* is always *bofome,* and pagination is sometimes whimsical (Craze: "One is to assume that the printers went out to lunch at that point and had a bit to drink"). In Shakespeare's day—regardless of what you saw in *Shakespeare in Love*—acting troupes sometimes performed a new play a day, and thus actors were often unable to rehearse. Moreover, they were given not complete scripts but, rather, cue scripts—only their own character's lines, preceded by the line of dialogue that was their cue. These cue scripts would come to the actors on rolled paper; they would roll out this paper—thus the word *role*?—to see how big their part was.

One dank, overcast Wednesday afternoon, Craze handed out cue scripts for the scene in *Romeo and Juliet* in which the two lovers are found dead—a scene of tumult and many, many exclamation points—and told us to memorize our lines overnight. I was cast as Capulet; I was to enter and say, "What should it be that they so shriek abroad?" then, at some indeterminate length of time later, I was to say:

O heavens!
O wife, look how our daughter bleeds!
This dagger hath mista'en, for lo his house

Is empty on the back of Montague,
And is missheathed in my daughter's bofome!

I showed my cue script to Laura—a wisecracking senior at University of Chicago who would emerge as one of my favorites in the group. "Lotta exclamation points," she observed. "You better get a good night's sleep."

"Yes," I responded. "Much drama for me. And a bofome."

The next day, Craze had us perform the scene without giving us any blocking. He provided only these Elizabethan guidelines: "Move to the person you're speaking to or about. If you have lots of lines, move to center stage. Also, think of status. If you're a prince, move to center stage."

Chaos ensued. Cues were missed; the First Watch bumped into the Second Watch, engendering testiness and faint moaning. One of the Southern Californians, cast as Juliet, fell to her knees at one point and started clawing the ground, as if to demonstrate her region's fascination with nail care. When we were done, we had a lot of questions for Craze. For instance, what would the Elizabethan actor who played the friar have done? Just after the friar enters, the Third Watch says, "Here is a friar that trembles, sighs, and weeps." Should the friar, upon hearing this description, heed it? Craze said yes. Wouldn't his walking out straight-faced and then, on cue, suddenly trembling, sighing, weeping, cause the audience to laugh?

"Indeed, it would."

Craze had us run the scene again. As we drifted to the back of the classroom, I asked Craze what an Elizabethan actor would do if, as had happened to me, his Capulet wasn't able to see Romeo's back—as Capulet's line, ". . . for lo his house/Is empty on the back . . . ," necessitated—because Romeo was lying on it. "Would the Romeo roll over?"

"Well, he can't really if he's dead, can he now?" Craze answered.

"I guess not."

"Maybe he kicks him right, or lifts him up."

I looked at Donald, who was playing Romeo, and said, "Face-down this time, Romeo, unless you want to be kicked into place."

The highly presentational nature of Elizabethan performance would again be impressed upon me the following week when Laura, Donald, and I went with two other classmates to the Globe Theatre to see *Henry V.* During Henry's marriage to Catherine of France, an audience member yelled out, "Don't do it!" whereupon Henry looked at her and said, "I'm sorry, madam, but I must."

⸻

FOR THOSE OF us who required lodgings, RADA had assigned some of us rooms in different dormitories within walking distance of Chenies Street; twelve or so others had been placed in a Middlesex Hospital dorm, alongside many young nurses; I was among this group. As I skulked down the hallway to the common bathroom each morning, the only male in sight amidst the many nurses swathed in bath towels, my breathing would suddenly sound very heavy to me, and my brain would flood with the ominous piano tinkling that is associated with the bad made-for-TV movie.

This aside, however, being in London for a whole month was not without a certain fabulous-getaway-vacation quality. No mail, no phone calls, all the enchantments of a world-class city before us—the possibilities staggered. My colleagues and I took in theater and art and movies; we tried to capture that most elusive beast, Swinging London. Early evenings typically found us at the Marlborough, the pub near school, where we were often hideously overserved.

When a group of summer students got together, the conversation often turned to our predecessors. As I lunched in the sparklingly clean RADA cafeteria with some of my fellow actors one day, Donald said, "You know, Joe Orton wasn't very happy while he was at RADA."

"Well, he met his boyfriend, Kenneth Halliwell, here—the one who killed him with a hammer," I pointed out. "That can be very trying on a relationship." Donald smiled. I asked, "Was Orton here for the full three years?"

"Only two."

"Gielgud was here only one year."

Who else had attended RADA, someone at the other end of the table asked. Who was the most notable graduate?

"Did Richard Burton go here?" Donald wondered aloud.

"Mmm, no."

"What about Larry? He's big."

"Larry O.?" I asked. "No Larry O. Kenneth Branagh, though. Anthony Hopkins, Peter O'Toole, Ralph Fiennes."

Donald widened his eyes. "They're big."

Tina joined in. "Juliet Stevenson and Glenda Jackson, too," she said.

"Mike Leigh, the director," I added. "And Marianne Jean-Baptiste, who was in *Secrets and Lies*. Umm . . . Jonathan Pryce. Fiona Shaw. John Hurt."

"Alan Rickman. Apparently he sits in on classes sometimes," Donald reported.

"Ohmygod, he is so sexy," Tina enthused. "I could not act."

"Albert Finney," Donald added. "Imogen Stubbs."

"I don't know who that is," I confessed.

"She's married to Trevor Nunn, the director."

Trevor Nunn: *Cats*.

I combed my mental files for more RADA alumni but found nothing. I remembered something else, though. "Did you know that when George Bernard Shaw died he left a third of his royalties to RADA?"

"Wow. No, I didn't."

"A cash cow. And Shaw—he has his own adjective. He has his own adjective, and it's one that requires special spelling. You can't get bigger."

"Total bigness."

Conversations like this buoyed our spirits and gave us the false impression that fame would be thrust upon us. Indeed, so galvanized was I by my talk with Donald and Tina that the following day I asked the charming and sheepish RADA stage-management student who was responsible for shepherding our group from classroom to classroom when we were likely to be graced with a visit from Alan Rickman.

"He doesn't sit in on summer-session classes," she explained. "He wants to watch people who are talented."

I LONGED FOR Craze's approbation. I took solace in the fact that the *Romeo and Juliet* exercise he had led us through had been too chaotic for him to use as a gauge of our talent. More telling would be the two projects he had in store for us—we were to do a condensed, workshop production of *A Midsummer Night's Dream,* to be presented on the penultimate day of class; we were each to leave the program with a modern and a classical monologue suitable for auditioning purposes.

Craze cast me as Oberon, *Dream's* king of the fairies. I love this character; I loved the part. Oberon is everything I am not—jealous, raging, highly sexed, otherworldly. The added bonus of the role was the frequency with which Oberon employs the term *love juice,* or, as I was saying it, "lohv joooz"; I found myself trying to get as much saliva as possible into vocal manufacture of this term.

Craze let each of us interpret our roles for ourselves; I saw Oberon as a sinister but elegant voluptuary with a ticking time bomb for a heart. You will nod emphatically, I think, when I tell you that chief among my favorite words in the English language is *slyboots;* I incorporated it in my interpretation, hoping it might impart a gliding, wafting quality to my movements.

In our first few rehearsals, I had trouble summoning the requisite anger toward Titania. But then I remembered once reading that if you have to play drunk onstage, you don't play the drunkenness, you play the trying-not-to-appear-drunkenness; this sidesteps cliché and generalized behavior. So I decided to play trying-not-to-strangle-Titania. This helped.

Midway through rehearsals, Craze asked me one day why Oberon was interested in the Indian boy, or the changeling. "I think Oberon wants to have his way with that little Indian boy in order to hurt Titania," I said, hoping Craze would find this daring.

Laura, sitting next to me, yelled, "Oh, stop! He's only a little boy!" Craze, however, accorded this interpretation his approval.

Later that day I found myself asking Craze why Oberon, whose jealousy and petulance ignites the motor of the play— the application of *lohv joooz* on Titania and the mortals—even bothers with the mortals. "What's in it for me?" asked this Oberon.

"Compassion," Craze said. "And then you'll do the love juice on Titania, which will lead you ri—"

"*Right* into pederasty," I finished his sentence.

Craze smiled slyly as Laura started yelling, "Stop! This is upsetting me!"

At lunch in the cafeteria a few days later, I found myself explaining my interpretation of Oberon to one of the actors from another group. "Intense," he commented. "And how old do you see the boy as?"

"About four," I answered. "But he has the *body* of a six-year-old."

As the rehearsals went along, I also tried to play up the lustful ardor that Oberon has for Titania. I caressed, I nuzzled. One morning one of the Helenas (because we had ten women in the class, some of the roles were double-cast) commented, "You're finding a lot more sex in Oberon."

"Oh . . . thanks," I said, slightly embarrassed. "But I hope it's not getting too . . . crotch-based?"

"I think you're okay," she said reassuringly.

But was I becoming too earnestly thespian outside of class? One Friday, Tara, a young woman in my group, asked me if I was planning on seeing either of the two upcoming student productions of *The Tempest* or *Macbeth.*

"Probably not *The Tempest,*" I said, "but I'll probably go to the Scottish play."

"The Scottish play?" she asked satirically.

I explained that it has long been considered bad luck for actors to refer to *Macbeth* by name, and that, historically, productions of the play are cursed by disaster and death.

"Yes, I know this. But you're only supposed to avoid saying the name if you're *in* the play," Tara pointed out.

"I don't want to take any chances."

Tara rolled her eyes heavenward. "Oh, give me a break."

I WAS WORKING on two monologues. My contemporary one was from a one-man show called *Furtive Nudist* by the British monologuist Ken Campbell: a shy man at the beach is addressed by an impatient overhead God, who badgers him into going skinny-dipping. My classical piece was Lucius, Titus Andronicus's son, drenched in "oblivion and hateful griefs," saying good-bye to his father and his sister, Lavinia, and vowing revenge on the men responsible for raping her and then cutting off her tongue and hands and for messengering Andronicus his own hand and the heads of two of his other sons. (Long story.)

Craze met with us in our classroom twice individually to

work on our monologues. In our first session together, I told him, "I read that Peter Brook's production of *Titus Andronicus* was so upsetting that they had an ambulance outside the theater to take audience members to the hospital."

"Yes," Craze said, eyes twinkling. "It's a *wonderful* play for a director."

In our second session he decided that as Lucius I should pantomime touching my father and sister as I bid them leave. "I think you want to put your hands on your father's shoulders." He demonstrated. "Then go to Lavinia and take her hands—"

"Unh, she doesn't have any hands."

"Right, right. So maybe shoulders again."

CRAZE HAD ENCOURAGED us to invite people to our workshop production (no scenery, no costumes) of *Dream*.

"And if you want to invite aunties with a lot of money so you can say, 'Here's how much I've progressed, just imagine how much better I could be after three years at RADA,' you can."

My boyfriend, Jess, was going to be in London during part of the final week of the program, so I figured I would make him watch either the dress rehearsal or the performance.

But there was a second person I hoped to lure. I skittered down to the main lobby during lunch on the Monday of our last week and found Val, the wonderfully warm and slightly frazzled-looking receptionist in her late forties. Val would often greet you in the morning by asking, "Have you got your badgie, dearie?" referring to our RADA ID cards; she, along with Ken Black, RADA's box office manager, was the individual to whom one posed any query or request of an administrative or logistical nature. I approached Val at her desk; her large eyeglasses magnified her already intense eyes.

"What exactly is Her Majesty the Queen's relationship to the school?" I asked, having seen the Queen listed as "Patron" on all official RADA documents. "Would it be possible to get her to a summer-session class presentation?"

"Oh, I don't think so, love," Val said, slightly apologetically.

"No?"

"I don't think so," she reiterated. "Diana used to come."

"She did?"

"She was president, right after John Gielgud. You'd be amazed by all the security we had to go through."

I nodded sagely, looking down at the floor. I asked, "But what do you think would get the Queen's fanny in a seat—refreshments? Bourbon?"

Her face registering a note of alarm, Val said, "I'll show you a picture of my daughter meeting the Queen."

I moved closer to her, and we gazed in unison at the color photograph.

"That's wonderful," I gushed.

"You can imagine I have it in a much larger version at home."

"The billboard version," I mused.

She smiled. When the moment had passed, I said, "So, our *Midsummer Night's Dream* is on Thursday at four o'clock, on the second floor."

A note of exasperation creeping into her voice, she gazed at me indulgently and said, "I'll tell Ken you want the Queen to come."

I thanked her.

....

ALL OF THE Shakespeare in my head—Oberon, Lucius, fragments of dialogue from class exercises—was starting to blur. Although I was the first person in our group to learn all his lines for *Dream,* it did not necessarily follow that I was the person with the best command of his lines. I could almost always remember the beginning of my speeches, but by the fourth or fifth line, a haze sometimes descended.

"Unh, you're not quite following the text," Craze told me at a rehearsal one day.

"Sorry."

"But, strangely, you *are* staying in meter."

"Which is, of course, far more important than actual meaning," I vamped.

Craze looked at me skeptically.

I kept returning to the script, kept reciting my lines to the wall of my dorm room.

At one of our last rehearsals, Craze reported, "Henry, you've gone off on your own tangent a few times again."

Uh-oh.

Craze said, "You win the Fakespeare Award."

WE PERFORMED *DREAM* in a nearby park; it went quite smoothly, and fourteen people attended. Upon its conclusion, there was hugging and kissing and a general air of bonhomie.

"How did your presentation go?" a RADA student asked me in the pub that night.

"I think the word is *searing*," I said.

Jess had watched our dress rehearsal and had congratulated me, but I wasn't sure what he really thought of my performance. So I asked him what he would have changed. "I would have had you do it in your own voice," he said.

"Oh, you mean because I was doing that sort of low-pitched, mysterioso number with my voice?"

"Yes," he responded. "But I would have kept all the facial expressions."

Facial expressions?

"My good man," ran the response that my synapses started forming, "that was no mere series of facial expressions but rather the living, breathing embodiment of psychological nuance and shading that is the result of the kind of all-encompassing rehearsing that can only proceed upon the completion of copious textual analysis."

Then I thought: don't say this.

――――――――

THE NEXT MORNING, back in the classroom, we all performed our monologues for one another. My Lucius came off haltingly and unevenly; but my shy man at the beach got a lot of laughs. Laura came up to me afterward and said, "Hank, your Furtive Nudist rocked." Relief.

But we still had our exit tutorials with Craze to come. After lunch we discovered that our leader had hung up a list of appointment times on the door of our classroom.

"Wait a minute," I said as three of us perused the list. "Peter, Tanya, and I all have twenty-minute appointments. Everyone else's is only ten minutes."

I made the assumption that a longer appointment would be required for the shattering of illusions—say, seven minutes for the messenger of the bad news to back slowly into the bad news, two minutes for the recipient of the bad news to be defensive and unpleasant; one minute for the messenger to say, "There, there" and to suggest that, after all, his is only one opinion among thousands, other people might tell you differently, I mean, look at Arnold Schwarzenegger, someone keeps hiring *him*; ten minutes for the non-Schwarzenegger entity to weep openly.

Some of us sat in the hall outside the classroom in clumps of two or three; others took to the streets in order to dissipate anxiety by means of heavy snacking.

The first few evaluees emerged from their appointments unscathed and told of being encouraged to keep studying, keep working. Then one emerged brimming with tears; her eyes trained on the floor, she walked off without talking to any of us.

I was the first twenty-minute appointment. As I sat on the floor, I closed my eyes and tried to relax. My head was an echo chamber: "Henry has a lot of tension in his upper lip . . ." "You've gone off on your own tangent a few times again . . ." "You would be perfect for Osric, Hamlet's effeminate courtier."

The door opened. Tara motioned me inside. Craze was seated. I sat opposite him.

"Here is your diploma," he said, handing me a certificate. I thanked him. "What did you hope to accomplish with this course?" he asked me calmly.

I explained that I wanted to be able to perform Shakespeare such that people could follow my meaning. To my mind, there are two kinds of Shakespeare actors—those whose speeches I can follow, and those who may or may not be saying, "And so in aspic do we gavotte . . ."

"Well, I certainly think you did that."

I thanked him.

He suggested that I continue training. "It's mostly a question of the voice," he said. "It's still whiny and gets lost in the jaw a bit."

"Right."

"But I think you're doing some nice character work. I thought some of your Oberon was quite fun and daring."

"Oh, thank you," I said, genuinely grateful, a little surprised.

"As a director, I think that if you were willing to do smaller roles at your age, I'd be willing to take you in."

Cue trumpets.

ON MY LAST night in London I drank a contemplative beer with Thomas, a fellow summer student I had met in my dorm.

We had been talking about Baz Luhrmann's film version of *Romeo and Juliet*, with Leonardo DiCaprio and Claire Danes, which we had both liked.

"When I get home," Thomas said, "I'd really like to do a modern-day version of *Julius Caesar* but set it in the world of high finance."

"Sounds interesting," I said.

"What about you?"

"I've always wanted to stage *Two Noble Kinsmen* inside a blast furnace and call it *Chernobyl Kinsmen*."

"Wow."

"Yeah."

Our futures seemed rosy. Anything could happen. And probably would.

CHAPTER 2

*I*F THERE WAS anything that my sojourn at RADA had given me, it was a veneer of respectability. I hid under this veneer upon returning to New York. When people asked me about my stay in London, I did not tell them that the summer session is considered somewhat lightweight or that it does not require an audition; rather, I would simply drop the name Royal Academy like I was drawing a gun. It worked—people froze.

Except my friend Bruce. When I told him that I had spent the summer studying Shakespeare in London because I wanted to do more performing, he said, "Eccch. *Why?*"

I reminded him that I had done a fair amount of performing as a youth and was eager to do more. Two days later, while Bruce and I were standing in line to buy movie tickets, the topic came up again.

"How long are you going to live *that* lie?" Bruce asked.

"I realize the idea is wholly unpalatable to you," I said.

"You're not kidding."

I felt tears well up in my eyes and, once in the theater's lobby, quickly excused myself to use the bathroom in order to save face.

That I would not talk to Bruce for almost two years after this incident—when, ironically, Bruce would see me on TV and immediately call me, blurting excitedly, "You're on TV!"—only supported my thesis that few professions encapsulate Americans' ugly fixation on status more glaringly than acting does.

Well, I guess it could have been worse, I thought, as I lurked in the movie-theater bathroom after Bruce's comments. Thank God I didn't have to tell him that I want to be a mime.

CHAPTER 3

*M*Y FRIENDS' AND COLLEAGUES' reactions to my next the-atrical venture all fell within that narrow band of the emotional spectrum that authorities would probably label "intense disbelief." One asked, "You're taking *your mother* to improv camp?" Another put it, "You're taking your mother to *improv camp*?" It was unclear which was more disquieting to them—that, while trying to hone my improvisational skills, I would be weighted down with an extra appendage in the form of my sixty-nine-year-old bird-watching, chain-smoking mother, or that I would be exposing this same untrained talent to the rigors of taking suggestions from an audience and talk-ing with a phony French accent.

The workshop I had found was run by Paul Sills. Profes-sional improvisational theater as we know it today was born in 1955 when Sills and some of his colleagues from the University of Chicago started the Compass Players; the Players then went on to start The Second City, of which Sills was the original di-rector, honing the burgeoning talents of the young Mike Nichols, Elaine May, and Alan Arkin. Now a teacher as well as director, Sills offers a three-hundred-dollar weeklong improv intensive each summer at his farm in beautiful Door County, the peninsula that juts out into Lake Michigan north of Green

Bay; the workshop concludes in Sills's barn with a Saturday-evening performance for an invited audience.

I had thought to ask my mother along for two reasons. First, she is a source of much mirth who has, on several occasions, accompanied me on my participatory journalistic forays and, in so doing, displayed a ready store of comic aplomb; it seemed only natural that our future collaborations would benefit from a little, ahem, *training.*

Second, I had been moved to include my mother because of Sills. He is probably the only person in show business whose biography always mentions his mother. Sills's bio in the brochure of the New Actors Workshop, the school founded by Sills, Mike Nichols, and director George Morrison, where Sills still teaches, starts with the sentence "Paul Sills is the son of Viola Spolin and has been active in improvisational theater all his life." The late Viola Spolin is the author of what many consider the bible of improv, *Improvisation for the Theater,* a compendium of theater games she devised while working for Northwestern University–based sociologist Neva Boyd; Sills, having been trained in these games from an early age, is now considered the foremost exponent of his mother's work.

And so I was moved to invite my own mother to join me for the workshop. After all, hadn't I, too, grown up tugging on my mother's comedic apron strings? Wasn't I, too, the foremost exponent of her improvisational "work"? (Mom is a retired social worker; her most notable theatrical outing was her brief stint as a greeter at the colonial reconstruction Old Sturbridge Village, where not a few tourists have probably become confused when they looked out their bus's windows into the parking lot and saw a chain-smoker in a mob cap.)

I called her. Mom seemed enthusiastic about the idea of studying with the original director of Second City; when I explained that I would be writing about our experiences just as I had when we had worked on magazine articles, she exhibited her somewhat tenuous grasp of Yiddish by responding, "Oh, so it's our usual stick."

She asked about the nature of the theater games we would be playing in the workshop; I explained one called Contact. "You improvise a scene," I said, "but every time you say something you have to justify touching your scene partner."

A pause.

She offered, " 'You have a little piece of spinach on your shirt.' "

I sensed that Mom would be using the workshop to work through her complicated relationship with dry cleaners.

I TYPED UP a résumé for Mom, highlighting the more performance-based aspects of her eighteen years as a social worker ("conducted many home visits") and her briefer tenure at Sturbridge Village ("greeted visitors while wearing mob cap"). I sent this résumé, along with my own, off to Sills. Because Mom has remarried, we don't have the same last name, so I wrote on our application, "Ann Earley is my mother."

A month later Sills's wife, Carol, sent me a postcard saying Mom and I had been accepted. Accommodations had been secured for us at a local guest house; Carol wrote that the guest house had a "marvelous bathroom." I called Mom, who was excited and who expressed a heretofore-suppressed desire to portray Queen Victoria. We then both speculated as to the potential marvels of the bathroom.

Indeed, after we flew to Green Bay and then drove an hour north to Door County, Mom's and my first instinct, upon arrival at our lodgings, was to surveil the vaunted bathroom. Large and very tidy, it had as its distinguishing feature two showerheads that projected straight down from the ceiling over the tub.

"What do the two showerheads mean?" Mom asked me.

I did not know. Ten minutes later, when Rick, the charming and boyish proprietor of the guest house, came to help us settle in, Mom reiterated, "What do the two showerheads mean?"

Rick replied, "Well, it's for a . . . *larger* experience." Mom looked at me questioningly. I returned this look.

I asked Rick, "Is this a shower for fat people?" He insisted that it was not.

THE NEXT MORNING Mom and I drove to Paul Sills's farm, where we met him and Carol. Paul, whose sandals and shock of grayish white hair give him the air of a bohemian, avuncular Anthony Hopkins, corralled us thirteen players into the barn, where, on a wooden platform some thirty feet square, we would be playing Viola's games for five hours a day. "We have a diverse group," Paul told us once we were all assembled on wooden benches. "There's a married couple, there's a mother and son." The group also included three drama majors, two professional actors, and four drama teachers, one hailing from Japan.

Many of the exercises and games that Sills led us through dealt with creating "a Where," or a specific theatrical reality. To create a Where you have to locate and interact with imagined objects within the Space.

"Just reach out in front of you and feel an object," Sills said to us at one point early on. Mom reached out in front of her and started gently swishing her hands around as if in the pre-soak phase of a manicure. Sills looked at her and said, "You need to feel it in Space."

"I am," Mom said.

"But what's there?" he asked, scowling.

"You can't tell something's there?" Mom asked.

"No."

"It's an organdy doily."

Sills looked unimpressed.

During a ten-minute break, we drifted outside the barn into the yard, some of us clumping around the picnic table. "It's so wonderful that you and your mother came to this together," one of the players, a cheery drama teacher from the Midwest, said to me.

I replied, "Mom is especially excited about playing Contact and has some very interesting ideas about touching." She nodded uncertainly.

Alas, we never got to play Contact, one of Spolin's best-known games. Indeed, Sills's approach could be unpredictable. He told us repeatedly that he did not want us to try to be funny or to engage in what he called "playwriting"—creating plot. He wanted us to "enter the Chekhovian space," to "embrace metaphor." In one game, we were paired up, and then one scene partner would leave the room. Upon reentering, the scene partner, judging solely by the way his colleague was treating him, would try to guess the Where and the Who (the location and the players' relationship to each other) that his colleague had predetermined.

When my partner, Bill, had left the room, I told the class that Bill was an organ donor whose organ donation had saved my life; unwittingly, he was about to check into my bed-and-breakfast. I thought this scenario had rich comic and dramatic potential. But Sills said to me, "Where will that get you? He'll just spill it out of you, and then there'll be a lot of playwriting and it will go on and on." Sills suggested that I make Bill my grandfather and that we be at a barbecue. I heeded this suggestion.

Hoping to veer away from the potentially maudlin, I tried to inject the scene with zest by making my character slightly urban and sarcastic ("Want some chicken? Don't let the char scare you—that's your flavor"). The scene seemed to go fairly smoothly, even if it was not a laugh fest. Later, during a break, one of my colleagues complimented me on the scene. I thanked her, and explained that when the TV show *Rhoda* first started taping, Second City alum Valerie Harper had the *Rhoda* cast play all of the Viola Spolin games in order to create a feeling of ensemble. "So I was doing that scene *as* Valerie Harper," I said. She applauded this effort.

From time to time, I worried that Mom wasn't having enough fun in the workshop. Sills could be very sweet to her ("I think he's disarmed by you," one player said to Mom. "No one else does exactly what you do the way you do it.") Many people in the group were having difficulty with Sills's impatience and with his frequent failure to clearly explain the rules of the individual games; it seemed only natural that this would be exacerbated by Mom's lack of improv experience.

But she soldiered on.

Sills was difficult to please. Mom did a scene one day in which she lost her wedding ring in the kitchen sink; Sills stopped Mom and her scene partner, saying it was all too evident that losing the ring had been planned ahead. "You're just two characters," he said. "It's just Mike and Elaine. Not actors, not playwrights. It's just Mike and Elaine." During another game—one called Stage Picture—Sills stopped Mom and me and the four other actors on the stage and, hoping to bring more truth to our work, had us "do some Space"—walk around, letting the air in front us whoosh through our bodies. Then he had us start up Stage Picture again, prompting Mom to ask him, "Are we still fluidizing our bodies?"

"No, nothing spiritual for you, dear."

⸻

THAT NIGHT, OVER a hand of Crazy Eights in our room, I asked Mom, "How's it going for you? Are you hanging in there?"

"The people are lots of fun," she said. "I really like that Janet."

"Me, too. But you're doing okay with the games?"

"I'm not always understanding what he wants."

"I know what you mean."

I suggested that by the performance on Saturday, we probably would have played each game three or four times and thus would feel more secure about each game's rules and mandate.

"Oooh, the performance," Mom half-said, half-moaned. "I'm not looking forward to that."

WHEN PAUL HAD to go to the dentist one morning, Carol took the reins of the workshop for him. Warm but soft-spoken, and dressed in jeans and a work shirt, Carol nimbly led us through a series of games. Later that afternoon I fell into conversation with her near the picnic table during a break.

"When Viola was alive," I asked her, "did she and Paul actually teach classes together?"

"Not really. She would do classes at Second City, and he would be there."

"I'm really interested in Paul's and my mother's commonality."

"You obviously have a good relationship with your mother."

"Yes. But always: slight tension."

"People would give Paul a hard time and say, 'What's it like working with your mother?' But to him it wasn't like that, it was like working with this theatrical genius who just happens to be your mother."

I nodded sagely, empathetically. "Mom is doing really well so far," I offered.

"I can see. I was watching yesterday."

"She doesn't have a lot of experience. But she gets right in there. She has a slightly manic quality reminiscent of the young Alan Arkin."

Carol paused to consider this last statement. She concluded, "It's true."

....

THE FOLLOWING DAY Sills taught us to play What's Beyond: having agreed on an incident in the past that directly affects how they treat each other in the present, two players improvise a scene; the audience tries to figure out what the incident was. Tanya, my scene partner, whispered in my ear, "We lost a baby." We launched into a somewhat maudlin scene about gluing photos in a family album; Sills stopped us about a minute into it. He told us to tell everyone what our incident had been; we did. Sills rattled off some possible suggestions: "Maybe you just moved into the apartment. Maybe you just had a big fight. Or maybe you're not married." At this last suggestion, Mom, seated next to Sills, blurted out, "Oh, but they *are*—that baby wasn't illegitimate!"

I felt my cheeks flush slightly as the class erupted into laughter.

At the picnic table during the next break, the cheery drama teacher from the Midwest sidled up to me and said, "Henry, we all just love your mother."

"She's good, isn't she?" I said.

"An inspiration."

Later that day Sills introduced a game called Slow-Fast. "It's torture," he said, "but let's do it. Viola's last words on her deathbed were 'Slow-Fast.' It's important." Slow-Fast turned out to be nothing more than a scene that, at the behest of an offstage arbiter, is intermittently launched into slow or fast motion. Mom and two other women decided to play sisters who were washing a car; when an argument erupted, Mom crawled under the car and, lodging herself there, had to be dragged out in slow motion. The scene produced gales of laughter and was subsequently cited by Sills three times as an example of the kind of work he was hoping would emerge from the workshop.

"Mom, you killed!" I gushed after the scene.

"Oh, thanks," she muttered.

"There's a new star in the comedy firmament tonight."

"Sure, sure."

"I think the two most exciting words in show business are *Ann Earley*."

She chuckled. I asked her about her "process."

"Well, I was just, you know, doing what seemed real," she said.

"Darling, I wish I could bottle that realness and sell it on Wilshire Boulevard."

I HADN'T TALKED much with Sills, so during a break, seeing him fixing a cup of coffee at the far end of the barn, I joined him.

"It's interesting that we've both worked with our mothers," I said, pouring some milk into a cup of coffee.

"Where did you work with yours?" he asked.

"Well, I mean, mostly in this workshop."

"Oh, right."

"But I guess that I, like you, am trying to interpret my mother's theatrical legacy."

Sills nodded reluctantly. "It can be powerful. Obviously, there's a strong emotional tie between parents and children. It's a commandment in the Bible, too—'Honor thy father and mother.' "

"Right," I said, pausing to stir my coffee. "I think Mom is doing really well so far."

"She's obviously very intelligent."

"Yes. And as a performer she has an engaging manic quality."

He blinked.

"Mamet quality?" he asked.

Suddenly imagining Mom in a sharkskin suit yelling, "Fuck the contract!" I reiterated to Sills, "Manic."

"Oh, yes. Lots of energy."

"But I guess that if you work with your mother a lot, you run the risk of being called a mama's boy."

"Oh, that doesn't matter. I never cared about that."

AS OUR SATURDAY-NIGHT performance loomed ever closer, Mom became increasingly anxious. Paul told us that thirty or so people who lived in the area would attend; we would play about an hour's worth of games and scenes using audience suggestions, and then cake and wine would be served. "I'm trying not to think about tomorrow," Mom told me over a dinner of whitefish, the local specialty, on Friday. In an attempt to allay her fears I reminded her how well-received her crawling-under-the-car scene had been. "Well, I can't crawl under a car in every scene," she said.

"No," I agreed. "That would start to look a little desperate." She also expressed concern that the audience would get bored during what was to be the final game—Transformations. In Transformations, an increasingly large group of players mirror one another's sounds and movements; each player tries not to initiate anything but rather to expand on the others' lead. The result is a primordial soup—if one actor starts scratching, then everyone starts scratching; then someone complains about the bugs, prompting the group to start slapping themselves and one another; a fistfight commences; the fistfight turns into a ballet sequence, and so on. It was wildly fun to do, similar to flight. But Mom, who had sat on the sidelines for two rounds of the game, had pronounced it sluggish viewing.

Had success spoiled Ann Earley?

FOUR HOURS LATER we drove over to Sills's barn. I had tried to allay Mom's apprehension by initiating a massive session of Crazy Eights, with betting. For me, the fact that I would probably never see any of the audience members again in my life was hugely relieving; my emotional state was tingly but not over-wrought. But when Mom and I got into the car, her anxiety was palpable. After a tense three-minute silence, she spoke up. "Worst-case scenario: diarrhea?"

"That could be bad," I allowed.

We whizzed by several motels, a patch of forest.

She continued, "Or vomiting." She paused to collect her thoughts and concluded, "Anything out of any orifice."

I considered her thesis.

"Worst-case scenario," I offered.

"Yes."

"Arrive twenty minutes late. Commence projectile vomit-ing."

"Oh, yes. Yes. There you go."

Fortunately, what we feared did not come true. About twenty-five friendly-looking people showed up to watch us. Paul, in his inimitably charming but rambling manner, emceed the evening; he explained that the games were created by Viola Spolin, but he did not mention that he was her son. He intro-duced the first game and said to Mom, who was seated alone on a bench, "If I could ask you for your seat, Ann." Mom stood, and starting off into the audience, said, "I'll just go home." Her tone was not exactly clear. I had a moment of panic. Was she walking? Was this Mom's answer to Stella Adler breaking off from the Group Theatre? Would Sills be moved to yell, as direc-tor Joseph L. Mankiewicz had to Katharine Hepburn on the set of *Suddenly, Last Summer,* "We will resume shooting, Miss

Hepburn, when the Directors Guild card which I ordered for you arrives from Hollywood"?

"Why don't you sit on this bench, dear," Paul said, pointing to a bench on stage left. Mom did. She was smiling. I experienced sudden relief.

The performance went smoothly, eliciting a wealth of mid-sized laughs. Mom was fairly restrained in her stage time, volunteering herself for only two games; sadly, she and I did not get to work any of our magic together. I played Explore and Heighten with Ned—you do a scene about a suggested topic (in our case, planning a funeral), while a side coach tells you to "explore!" or "heighten!" various moments, thus giving license to exaggeration. When told to explore the chair I was sitting in, I became wriggly and preorgasmic; this was thoroughly enjoyable and yielded a fair amount of audience reaction.

After our performance the players and the audience intermingled, reveling in the pleasures of cake and wine. Rick, the proprietor of our lodgings, rhapsodized to Mom, "Ann, you have a mesmerizing voice. It's low and modulated. Beautiful." Several minutes later, spying me standing alone, he walked up to me and told me, "Henry, I *really* like your mother. Don't be made uncomfortable by that."

"Okay," I said tentatively.

Feigning desire for a piece of cake, I bade Rick good-bye and positioned myself on the other side of the barn, hoping that my solitary state would spur on the advance of a fan.

But: nothing.

In fact, I soon found myself talking to a local craftswoman who, having heard that I had attended the workshop with my mother, wanted me to point Mom out to her. I did; a small circle of admirers had gathered around Mom, who was holding forth over near the picnic table.

"Quite the little fan club," the craftswoman noted.

"Well, just remember," I said, a twinge of jealousy starting to percolate within me, "Wisconsin had a *long* winter this year."

Where were my fans? The only person who appeared to have any reaction to my work was, not surprisingly, Mom. She told me she had enjoyed the scene in which I planned a funeral and "explored" my chair.

"That was funny," she said.

"But . . ." I tried to anticipate the rest of her thought.

"But I was a little worried that you might get an erection."

I assured her that this possibility had been altogether remote.

Once the bulk of the audience had dispersed, Paul and Carol, all of the players, and some friends and family sat at the picnic table for an hour or so. We reminisced, swapped phone numbers, and promised to keep in touch.

———

ON THE PLANE back to New York, Mom and I shared our impressions of the workshop and performance. I congratulated her again.

"You were a big hit," I said.

"You think?"

"Absolutely."

She smiled and settled into her seat to fall asleep. As she drifted off, I stared at her. One part of me thought, I hope that I'm as game and energetic and fun when I get to be her age.

But the other part wondered, What does she have that I don't?

CHAPTER 4

*I*N THE ACTING PROFESSION, as in life, you must make the most of your tiny allotment. He who waits until he has been cast as Othello to pull out all the stops is setting himself up for disappointment—it will be Othello, not Desdemona, who is strangled in this production. So when a classmate told me she was helping to cast extras for the remake of *Godzilla,* I quickly recommended myself for duty. I clearly had not slayed them at improv camp in Wisconsin; here was an opportunity to channel my feelings of disappointment into bravura acting. And perhaps, in so doing, to achieve every extra's dream: to be awarded a line of dialogue.

My classmate called me two days later and said that the filming, to be done that Sunday, would involve prodigious amounts of stage rain. I assured her that I was no stranger to adverse meteorological conditions, natural and man-made, and, as such, could "play wet." The pay for non–Screen Actors Guild talent was seventy-five dollars; I needed to be available all day and night. I was to wear a London Fog–type raincoat and carry a black umbrella.

The harbinger of location shooting in a metropolitan area is a table on the sidewalk, heaped high with haggard bagels. When I arrived at the appointed location in the Financial District that Sunday morning at six-thirty, although the chaos I found there—Teamsters bickering over sports scores, thick black cables veining the streets as if to depict the late stages of arteriosclerosis—had all the earmarks of filmmaking, I did not see the telltale breadstuffs and so was moved to ask the first walkie-talkie–wielding individual I saw, "Where are the bagels?"

"Are you SAG or non-SAG?" she asked.

"Non."

"You're in the tent."

She pointed to a huge, dun-colored tent around which loitered hundreds of men and women, many of whom were also wearing London Fog–type raincoats and carrying umbrellas. "My *people*," I exclaimed. I walked over to the tent and, seeing a line formed at one of the twenty or so tables thereunder, queued up. Four minutes later the casting people had checked my name off on a list and I had been given a voucher, the form by which I would be paid.

All was actor-clogged; I could barely find an empty seat at a table. I was glad I finally did—we proceeded to wait for two hours. During this time, small groups of us were presented to a young, unshaven man from Wardrobe who was, by turns, exhausted and sniffy. He looked at the camouflage cap that the fortysomething gentleman ahead of me in line was wearing and said, "I don't know *anyone* who would wear that cap." Then he scanned me—that is to say, my tan raincoat, my black umbrella, and my wingtips encased in black rubbers—and yawned, "You're fine."

Shortly thereafter we were herded down to the set in groups of thirty or forty. The set was Federal Hall, the majestic site of George Washington's inauguration, rich in Corinthian columns and impressive stairways, which dead-ends Broad Street in the manner of a lion's gaping jaws. Halfway up its main stairs was a podium, festooned with red, white, and blue bunting and a sign reading RE-ELECT MAYOR EBERT. I wondered aloud, "Where's the reptile?"

The self-appointed expert in my group explained, "They're gonna blue-screen him in later."

We lined up on the sidewalk and then, one by one, walked through a small, cordoned-off area where a sweet, pale, bespectacled man was handing out props. It looked like about a third of the extras were being given still cameras and two thirds were being given placards reading RE-ELECT EBERT.

"I hope I get a camera," the woman standing behind me in line said.

Eager to be filmed shooting at Godzilla, I responded, "I hope I get a Taser."

Moments later I was handed three props—a fake 35-millimeter camera, a fanny pack, and a press badge. I looked at the badge. The first thing I noticed was that the photo on it was of the man who had just handed it to me. Hovering over the photo was the name Sean Haworth and the call letters WAQR. These call letters sounded more like radio than TV to me; but then why was I carrying a still camera?

Rather than let this seeming contradiction bother me, I decided to base my character interpretation on it. What if Sean Haworth labored under the impression that if he took a good-enough photograph it would be aired on the radio? Wouldn't this, character-wise, raise the stakes, and imbue him with the driven quality that makes for an interesting dramatic character? *Poor Sean,* you can almost hear the editorial staff at WAQR whispering over the water cooler. *If only he understood that ours is an aural medium.*

But five minutes later an assistant director who had assembled about a hundred of us in front of Federal Hall took away my camera.

"I based my character interpretation on that!" I exclaimed, hoping that this would translate to him as "Serious actor. Could handle a line of dialogue."

"I need it for up front," he reported tersely, then walked to the front of the crowd.

One of my fellow colleagues—a vivacious English as a Second Language tutor and sometime actress in her early thirties with whom I had fallen into conversation back in the tent—witnessed my loss of camera and counseled, "You were probably overpropped anyway."

"Yes," I responded, "my work was getting proppy."

We proceeded to work for almost eleven hours, lunch break included, on variations of a single shot. In it, about four hundred of us New Yorkers are standing in the rain, listening to Mayor Ebert (Michael Lerner) give a speech. All of a sudden, we hear a *thump*. Some of the crowd—those born between January and April, to be precise—look behind them, down Broad Street, whence the sound originates. The mayor continues to natter on when *thump!* May through August now look down the street, too, expressing restlessness, a sense of discomfort, the vague possibility that this little piece of earth they call their own will soon be rent asunder. Then seconds later a third *THUMP!*: Godzilla appears, causing the crowd, regardless of natal season, to shriek with abandon, perhaps to drop umbrellas or placards, and to run off in a prescribed direction.

Since I was born in February, my prescribed direction was straight ahead, up the thirty or so stairs of Federal Hall. So, hearing my *thump*, I would look behind me down Broad Street in highly nuanced, ever-burgeoning panic; erupt into a despair-tinged, Edvard Munch–calibre scream on hearing the third *thump*; run northward, negotiating my way through what was, by now, a very festival of bad acting; ascend the stairs two at a time; look behind me again while closing my umbrella (note the elegant adherence to decorum, even in the face of apocalypse); and then hurl my body against Federal Hall's massive stone doors in an attempt to gain entry.

I loved this work. I would be hard-pressed to recount any event from my personal or professional life that more accurately typified the phrase *crazy fun*. Yes, my colleagues and I encountered much wetness; the rain machines were assiduous in their ministrations. Moreover, no lines of dialogue were being doled out by the director or assistant directors. But the acting task at hand wedded blitzkrieg-strength drama with stuntman-strength athleticism and, as such, was wholly engaging. Screaming at full force in the canyons of Wall Street on a Sunday morning was particularly liberating. On the first few takes (by the end of the day we would do more than twenty) I would yell, "Oh, my God!" or "There he is!" By the eighth take I was screaming, "Here comes trouble!" By the late afternoon, punchy, I was shrieking, in an accent vaguely Caribbean, vaguely Cockney, "'Zilla monster ate me baby!" causing the self-appointed expert to glare at me and say, "Let's keep it real, huh?"

This statement might have chastened were it not for the other extras. Seldom have I seen such a preponderance of scenery-chewing; my colleagues' every utterance and movement seemed to offer ready proof that vaudeville is not dead. Several of the extras, in an attempt to make themselves noticed, would run directly *at* the camera. Another one, a tall, fifty-something woman who appeared to be a recent graduate of the Lucille Ball School of Clown Makeup, made such a spectacle of repeatedly dropping and then retrieving her umbrella that an assistant director was forced to take the umbrella away from her; the woman, divested of her gimmick, then devoted her energies to a veritable Oberammergau pageant of shrieking.

"That woman just screamed right in my eardrum," the ESL tutor told me between takes, motioning with her head toward the offender.

"Yes," I acknowledged, "her work is *particularly* broad."

Another extra, a burly gentleman in his mid-thirties, was vying for attention by collapsing on his backside midway up the stairs, his bent legs splayed open in the manner of a sleeping dog unembarrassed by the public display of his genitals.

"That's a nice little, unh, advertisement you've got going there," I said to this man as I walked down the stairs at the end of one take. He looked at me uncertainly and then expressed anxiety about people running over him—he might get trampled, or worse, his tramplers might obscure him from the camera's view.

"Oh, I wouldn't worry about that," I said in reference to his second anxiety. Pointing at his open legs I said, "That will read."

"You think so?"

"That will definitely read."

CHAPTER 5

"He's playing Krogstad at La Jolla!"

One night shortly after the *Godzilla* shoot, I found myself blurting out this somewhat airy and pretentious-sounding statement to Jess. I was referring to Bill, the actor who lives in the apartment directly over mine (Jess and I had always kept separate apartments), gushing over the fact that Bill was playing the plum role of Krogstad—the villainous bank clerk in *A Doll's House*—at the prestigious La Jolla Playhouse.

Days later, while talking to a young woman studying film at Columbia University, my mind drifted back to my own days as a film student, and soon I was formulating a second airy, pretentious-sounding statement: "I love three-camera production: you can shoot in real time!"

Thespian fervor was entering my bloodstream.

Everywhere I looked, it seemed, I detected signs of show business. One weekend Jess and I drove to northwestern Connecticut to visit our friend Mary for the weekend. On the way we stopped in New Preston, a small, New Englandy hamlet whose cuteness threatens to suffocate; the town appears to be nothing but overpriced antique shops. Jess and I were walking around, making disparaging comments, when we heard a quavering haloo across the parking lot.

"Do you guys know anything about cars?"

The distraught woman stood beside her Range Rover–type car. Dressed in a nightgown with a jacket thrown over it, she was fiddling with the vehicle's passenger door, which would not close. Jess valiantly stepped forward and, casting a diagnostic gaze at the offending lock part, solved the problem in 4.3 seconds; I meanwhile surveiled the interior of the car, which was fraught with many adorable Asian children. The woman thanked us profusely, rambling on about her lack of automotive-repair skills in a way that was not wholly intelligible.

As Jess and I walked back to our car, I asked him, "Did you see who that was?"

"Mia Farrow."

"Yeah. Wow. Neurotic."

"And deploying an interesting means to car repair."

I looked at him unsurely.

He explained, "Not *everyone* would stop in an antiques mall and flag down the first two homosexuals in sight."

CHAPTER 6

OME WITH ME now to a small, clammy room located in the basement of an apartment building on the Upper West Side. That bare bulb? The one that hangs down from the ceiling and provides the room's only illumination, giving all those within its purview the look of angry tiki gods? Ignore that. The pipe overhead from which drips an unknown substance that will, and does, burn through actors' clothing? That, too: please ignore. The doom-suffused teacher sitting over to one side, the one who just critiqued one actor by saying, "Danny, your voice sounds like something that happened in the barn one night. It's as flatulent as sitting on the porch after dinner"—I'm not going to tell you again, *ignore this stuff,* you're getting caught up in extraneous trivia, it's distracting you and starting to affect your work.

Here is the work. Sit opposite a fellow student, knees almost touching his. Put all your attention on him. Forget about yourself. Respond to him. Trust your response to him. The response will take the form of a sentence, repeated over and over by the two of you, and generated by whichever of you two is so moved.

And so I find myself staring deep into Danny's compassionate, brown eyes and, when his facial expression registers a slight air of menace, saying, "Is that a threat?"

"Is that a threat?" he responds.

"Is that a threat?"

"Is that a threat?"

"Is that a threat?"

"Is that a threat?"

"Mr. Know-It-All."

"Mr. Know-It-All."

"I didn't wound you."

"I didn't wound you."

This exercise is called the Word Repetition Game, and it is the cornerstone of the Meisner technique, the school of acting under which Sanford Meisner brought the Neighborhood Playhouse and his students Sydney Pollack, Robert Duvall, Joanne Woodward, Gregory Peck, et al., to prominence. (David Mamet also studied with Meisner, and not surprisingly, many view the fractured cadences and echoing nature of his dialogue as having grown out of the Word Repetition Game.) The gist of the exercise is to erode self-consciousness, a particular bugaboo of Meisner's, and one that he, like many, thought was the by-product of Lee Strasberg and the Method. "I told Lee that when he was alive," Meisner explains to one of his students in *Sanford Meisner on Acting*. "I said to him, 'You introvert the already introverted . . .' Needless to say, he didn't pay any attention to me, but that's the reason why I'm a better teacher than he was." Meisner disparages Strasberg freely in the book, later calling him a "terrible actor" and saying that if you want to "amuse yourself in a sickening kind of way," look at the list of Meisner's Neighborhood Playhouse graduates, and you'll be amazed at how many of them Strasberg later invited to the Actor's Studio and then claimed as his own.

I bring this rancor up not because I am enthralled by bitchiness expressed by one older, raspy-voiced, Jewish luminary of the theater, now dead, toward another—although let's be honest, who isn't?—but because, interestingly, the teacher I was currently studying with feels *he* is a better teacher than Meisner. Yes, Robert Patterson—a Meisner protégé who, adding his own spin to Meisner's work, has hung out his shingle and earned a reputation as the wayward son of New York's Meisner-trained teachers—said to my class one evening, "Sandy was the most important teacher of the twentieth century. But he wasn't the best. That's me."

I KNEW THAT there were sadists out there—teachers who would tell you to "lie on the cold cement floor, breathe in through your buttocks, and then *hold it*," only to leave you holding it, leave you hanging in the balance while, for the next twelve minutes, they alcoholically sort through a stack of papers and cat hair in search of the Pinter handouts.

I was trying to avoid these people.

And yet, at the same time, I wanted rigor, I wanted structure, and I didn't want to spend a huge sum of money. And so I found myself under the auspices of Robert Patterson.

I found Patterson hugely intimidating; seldom have I encountered an individual who radiates "troubled genius" with such intensity. A man of a certain girth, he has a large, round, perpetually scowling face that is swathed in a silvery beard and mustache: Papa Hemingway without all the goddamned whimsy.

Classes met twice a week, at night. They were inexpensive (seventy-five dollars a week) and, rarity of rarities, sometimes had as few as four people in them. Patterson claimed that I was the 179th person he'd interviewed for the class; two weeks later he claimed I was the 202nd. I was flattered, if doubtful.

The first six weeks were devoted entirely to repetition.

"So you're the big guy now?"

"So you're the big guy now?"

"So you're the big guy now?"

"So you're the big guy now?"

"I didn't do anything wrong."

"I didn't do anything wrong."

"Okay, stop," Patterson said to Sara and me after this particular exchange. A wave of distaste came over his face as if to signal the recent ingestion of a tainted clam. He stared at me and asked, "Are you involved in an emotion-based activity?"

"I'm not sure what you mean," I said.

"Are you in therapy?"

"No."

"Are you involved in some kind of self-help?"

"No."

He said that such activities develop bad instincts in actors, adding, "We're learning to be truthful under imaginary circumstances, not to wallow in our feelings."

I nodded. A pipe overhead creaked, and I could see that the actors seated in the "audience" were looking at Sara and me empathetically.

Patterson looked down at his class list.

"I see you live in a three-six-six telephone exchange," he said, referring to my Greenwich Village prefix. "That's the capital of people sitting around in cafés and having a lot of bullshit conversations about their feelings."

I wondered where this was going.

"Are you in Al-Anon or a Twelve-Step group?"

"No."

"Well, forget that shit if you are."

Noted.

Patterson did not seem wowed by my talent. He stopped me repeatedly during the repetition exercise, once to point at my partner and ask me, "Is he berating you?"

"Yes."

"So if he's berating you, what happens?"

"I want to berate him back."

"That's mirroring, not acting."

"But if someone says to me, 'Let's go!' my response typically is 'Okay!' "

Patterson's look of queasy irritation was that of someone who has taken a long ride in a small boat.

"I don't care if that's your response. If I came into this class and pissed on the floor and told you to smell it, is that teaching?"

The possibility that the acid from the overhead pipe might now be splashing into a pool of urine below was too much; my mind began to reel.

"Just because you feel something," he continued, "doesn't mean that that's a genuine response. That's just conditioning. You're overanalyzing. It's nouveau riche bullshit."

"Okay."

"You have no frame of reference for this work. Do you think you know about acting?"

"Unh, I guess not."

"I'm not here to develop Suzy Show Me actors. Are you sure you're not in a Twelve-Step program or any kind of self-help?"

"Yes."

"I'll know if you are," he said. "And you never worked professionally?"

"No. When I worked in casting, I got to read with actors sometimes."

"And you thought you were *better* than them."

"No, I thought it looked like fun."

"It is fun. Acting should be fun."

(Tense pause.)

(Tense pause.)

(Tense pause.)

If only to hear a voice in the room, I said, "Maybe we should just do it again."

Patterson, nostrils flaired: "I think *I* should be the judge of that."

At the next class, the dynamic was much the same. I tried to be spontaneous and impulsive while repeating sentences; Patterson would repeatedly stop us and provide commentary.

"When you said in the last class that you were trying to have a truthful response," he said to me, "that showed that you're overanalyzing. You have to work off the change in the other actor. Acting is tangible. Trying to have a truthful response is a downtown-sit-in-a-café-nouveau-riche-bullshit-therapy approach. It's bullshit dilettantism. Am I making myself clear?"

"Abundantly."

I tried again with a new partner.

"What are you doing up there?" Patterson asked, seconds into our exercise.

"I'm trying to . . . to do my thing," I said.

"You're trying to do *what*?"

"You've told us not to overanalyze what we're doing, and that if we're conscious of what we're doing, then it's probably not working."

"Right. But actors have a way of working that's unique to them."

(Tense pause.)

I asked, "What can I do to make myself better?"

"Nothing. There's nothing you can do. You just have to do the work. It's obvious that you've never learned a craft before."

IT WILL NOT surprise you, I think, when I tell you that Patterson's students, all in their twenties or early thirties, tended to be martyrs or followers. You had to love the pain, or the pain would choke you. The dank basement studio seemed a lair for masochism. Whenever I entered the classroom, I had the sense of entering a cult's headquarters: one actor, Sean, had almost always arrived as much as thirty minutes early and would say, "Hello, Henry" gravely, as if we were surgeons before a big operation or Puritan aldermen who had convened to discuss what punishment to mete out to old Mrs. Emmett, who had tried to magick a wheelbarrow into a mule.

You had to thrive, too, on the cultural badgering—the reading list that Patterson handed out at the beginning of classes was some five pages long; the first ten minutes of each class saw him rattling off films and cultural events that he expected us to attend. "You have to develop taste," he told us. "You have to come to the conclusion that Laurence Olivier, despite his reputation, was a hack, while Oskar Werner was a great actor." (Oskar Werner played Jules in *Jules and Jim*.) Special attention was paid by Patterson to the cultural offerings of his former students, particularly Ted Danson and JoBeth Williams, whom we were to indulge for sometimes acting in projects not commensurate with their talents. (Of one Danson vehicle, Patterson said, "It's like Mozart at a Monkees concert.")

One night Patterson asked Kris, a sweet, birdlike dancer in her early twenties, who her favorite dancer was. When Kris faltered, unable to produce an answer, Patterson told her and three other students to stand in the middle of the room. "What's your favorite Verdi opera, non-Shakespearean?" he asked them, to resounding silence. Two of the four looked down at the floor, ashamed. "Shakespearean?" he asked. No answer. "What are your favorite James Stephens novels? He's the one who Joyce said should finish *Ulysses*. I thought you said you liked *Ulysses*," he added, looking at Kris. "You've got to talk your bullshit. Your favorite Faulkner novels? Austen novels?"

"*Pride and Prejudice*," Kris said.

"Favorite Ferlinghetti poems?"

This drill, which Patterson ran three times during the ten weeks I studied with him, was torture to watch. I squirmed with pain. As if it weren't troublesome enough to see him link cultural illiteracy with shame, his conception of the canon was vast—one night he asked a group, "What are your three favorite Henry Hathaway films?" A distinct puzzler. (Known for his westerns and crime dramas, Hathaway directed, among others, *Of Human Bondage, The Sons of Katie Elder,* and *True Grit.*)

But his point was valid: young actors are, on the whole, one of the most culturally ignorant groups working in the arts. I asked Rick, one of the more outspoken students, if he thought Patterson's methods were manipulative. "A little, sure," he said. "But you've gotta know that stuff."

Moreover, Rick, like many of the others, saw Patterson's class as a form of professional Darwinism: if they could withstand Patterson's abuse, surely they could withstand the vagaries of show business.

"HOW'S THE ACTING going?"

Mom had called.

"Pretty well," I told her. "I'm in a really difficult class right now."

"More difficult than Paul Sills?"

"Vastly."

"And what kind of stuff are you doing?"

"We repeat sentences."

"You repeat sentences?"

"We repeat sentences."

"Give me an example."

" 'We repeat sentences.' "

"And then I would say, 'We repeat sentences'?"

"You've obviously done this before."

AFTER I HAD been studying with Patterson for three weeks, he told me it was time to embark upon the two other prongs of my education: singing and dance. The instruction of the former fell to one Sonja Sorensen, a lovely, fey woman who gave lessons at the Ansonia, the huge, Beaux Arts building on Broadway and Seventy-third Street whose especially thick walls have made it a logical residence for people like Enrico Caruso and Arturo Toscanini, and earned it the nickname "the singer's ghetto." People who live in the Ansonia and who own a piano rent out their apartments by the hour to voice teachers.

Being in a stranger's apartment while the stranger was out had great voyeuristic appeal for me. I felt as if we had broken in and then, instead of stealing valuables, sung Cole Porter to the valuables. "Honey, something's wrong here," I could imagine a young wife telling her husband suspiciously as they entered their apartment late one evening. "Someone's been . . . someone's been singing 'You're the Top' to the sofa."

That I enjoyed singing show tunes as much as I did was a revelation to me. You see, I have always been made somewhat uncomfortable by the musical theater. While I wholly support the notion that certain occurrences in life will and should vault us over mere speech into beautiful song, I am made uneasy by any form of entertainment whose offerings exhibit such a predilection for the exclamation point. I am thinking here primarily of *Hellzapoppin'!* and *Whoopee!*, but I might just as well be talking about *Oklahoma!, Oliver!, Hello Dolly!, Over Here!, That Darn Cat!*, or, for that matter, any of the *Oh's—Kay!, Coward!, Captain!* or *Calcutta!*

The effect, overall: slight nervousness.

However, Sorensen was everything Patterson was not— wee, calm, and supportive—and so I was able to overcome my prejudices. Chief among her goals was to rid my voice of its gargly, *rrr* sound. When you sing, you are meant to sing the vowels, not the consonants; but when I sang, say, Porter's "So in Love," I had a tendency to sing, "Strrrange dearrr," instead of "Straaange deeear." Also problematic was my Cro-Magnon posture.

"Should I practice singing scales at home?" I asked Sorensen early on into our lessons.

"Yes," she replied. "And walk down the street looking *beautiful*."

The contrasting pedagogic approaches of Patterson and Sorensen could be schizophrenic. The day that Sorensen, praising me for hitting a particularly high note, exclaimed, "Yes, darling! And once you get there, *live* there!" was the same day that Patterson told me that I would never play King Lear because "it'd be like playing the *Emperor* Concerto on a Jew's harp." One hour Sorensen would be encouraging me to try to resonate a note in the tip of my "little chicken nose," and the next hour, two blocks away, Patterson would be bemoaning my "nouveau riche therapy bullshit."

But while my singing and acting lessons presented challenges, these challenges were as nothing compared to the Herculean rigors of the Martha Graham School of Contemporary Dance, where Patterson sent me for dance training. If, as Ben Franklin urged, we should beware any venture that requires new clothes, we should probably fall over dead if this activity requires that the new clothes be a leotard. All leotards should come with a label that reads, "Nothing good can come from this." But a leotard is a deceptive thing. At first blush, wearing one seems so energizing, not to say movement-producing: I am a watermelon seed, and the leotard is a thumb and index finger. "Stand back," my Danskin and I announce. "Flesh-rocket in transit."

I reported to the school's Upper East Side location. Upon

paying eighty-five dollars for a dance card good for ten dances, I was told that the school does not have an introductory class; you simply show up at any of the Level One classes offered during the week and then heave to. Although I am most inclined to allow memory to draw its gentle veil over all ten of my visits to the Graham school, I cannot; my first visit will remain with me always. My first class consisted of twenty-six dancers; at least a third of these appeared to be tiny Asian women, each with a waist the approximate width of a spaghetto.

I am no longer svelte; I have, with age, svelled. And so, nervously slipping into my black leotard and a black T-shirt in the men's changing room, I then skulked into the proper studio and sat on the floor behind all the other dancers. I scanned them for clues regarding preclass behavior: stretch out, repeatedly readjust leotard elastic to deter unattractive dimpling and waffling, yawn in bold expression of anorexia and/or boredom.

Suddenly the teacher—a tall, elegant German woman in her forties named Armgard von Bardeleben—arrived, causing all to stand. She encouraged us to spread out, sit, and then, with legs spread, collapse our torsos forward before sitting up slowly, building up our spines vertebra by vertebra. This was not too difficult and fairly relaxing. Then came a series of exercises in which, our legs in varying awkward configurations, we were to reach as far away as possible, dragging a hyperextended arm through the air slowly. These were nigh impossible to do. Moreover, upon looking at the other dancers, I could see that they were able to suffuse this activity with *tristesse*—they were swans, and they were perishing slowly within arm's reach of delicious foodstuffs.

"My young friend," Miss von Bardeleben said to me, lifting up my right leg, "Your legs are on de wrong zide, that is vhy it is zo hard for you."

I shifted my legs and tried again but sensed that this exercise required more of my lower back than my lower back was able to deliver.

Von Bardeleben walked back to the front of the class, saying, "And now, in double time! *Ein, zvei, drei!*"

My brain throbbed: lumbar nightmare.

The next forty-five minutes had us standing in order to perform a series of combinations in which we leapt, swiveled, flopped over, sprang back, kicked, reached, cowered, inflated, and collapsed. Many of these exercises were far beyond my comprehension, let alone my abilities; the one relief was that, as I was standing in the back row, the only people who could see me were von Bardeleben and her teaching assistant. At one point von Bardeleben came over to me and, gently laying a hand on my shoulder, said, "You must bend de knee, otterwise de head goes bananas from de shockink."

When the class approached its final half hour, von Bardeleben yelled out, "From de zide!" Everyone skittered over to the side of the studio. Von Bardeleben positioned herself in the middle of the room and showed us a combination that she referred to as "triple chassé sparkle sparkle": you take three running steps, then you leap in the air twice, lifting your arms up over your shoulders Evita-style to the left and then to the right.

I thought: No way. I *might* be able to fudge the triple chassé, but nothing about my skills is even remotely evocative of sparkling.

The class started lining up in pairs: we were going to triple chassé sparkle sparkle diagonally across the room, two at a time. We would all be able to see one another. Neatly dodging a cluster of tiny, perfect, Asian girls, I sidled up alongside a chubby woman in her forties. I gazed at her as if to say, "I love you." The pairs started peeling off, zipping across the room, a cavalcade of grace and vaulting; when the couple in front of us had completed their first sparkle, I took a deep breath and . . . then . . . off . . . I . . . went . . . *alone.*

The routine went off without a hitch, even if the vehemence with which I disported myself caused me to bump into the far wall several steps after my second sparkle. No matter. The routine was over. Done. As a reassuring air of completion settled over me, Tina, a nursery school teacher who had been taking classes at Graham for three years, said to me, "Guys are supposed to go last." I thanked her for this belated information. Seconds later, the last pair (the other two men in the class) flew across the room, and von Bardeleben walked over to the middle of the room to address the group.

"How many of you remember your first day?" she said, her right arm gesturing toward me. "Think back to that. He should not have to dance alone. No one should on their first day."

The group stared at me, all warm indulgence. The remainder of the class went more smoothly for me; however, it was clear to me that there will never be a PBS documentary about me that features a lot of baleful cello music and the title *Elusive Muse.*

I CONTINUED TO imbibe the powerful cocktail that was the Patterson-Sorensen-Graham trinity. Scheduling a singing lesson ("Yes, darling. Find the note and then nourish, nourish, nourish") directly before or directly after a Patterson ("You don't know anything about acting") or Graham class ("Right hand on hip, left leg up, and twirl") was a good way to soften these classes' blows; I never went to a Patterson and a Graham class on the same day, fearful that to do so would induce blithering.

The longer I studied with Patterson, the more his charms were thrown into high relief—the highs were higher; the lows were lower. In one class, when I told him that I was not an avid opera listener, he told me to buy a recording of Swedish tenor Jussi Bjoerling singing *The Pearl Fishers* duet; "It will change how you feel about opera," he said. I did, and wept upon hearing it, and I now include this recording among my most treasured possessions.

But Patterson's other pedagogical gambits grew increasingly disturbing to me. "Actors are assholes," he said to us one night, trying to explain how actors must be willing to make fools of themselves at any time. "Jack, go to the door," he said to one student. Jack walked over to the closed metal door. "Go through the door!" Patterson barked. Jack hurled himself frontally against the door. "See?" Patterson concluded. "Actors are assholes."

The final straw for me, however, came the night he critiqued Janet on the repetition exercise. Janet was a gorgeous, heavyset woman whom Patterson had held back twice, forcing her to duplicate months of classwork. He kept picking on her this particular night, interrupting her in mid-sentence and chastising her for appearing to be self-conscious. At one point he stopped her, saying, "Why do you do this?"

Janet gazed uncomfortably off into space, radiating shame.

"How blunt should I be?" Patterson asked.

"Very," Janet said.

"Well, you know how Irish I am."

"Yes."

"So don't be an Irish cunt."

Janet's eyes flooded with tears.

"Don't be a fucking lace-curtain Irish cunt."

CHAPTER 7

T WAS EASY to find other classes, and even easier to ratio-nalize staying in these classes rather than looking for work. In a soap-opera class at Weist-Barron School of Televi-sion, I was weekly afforded the opportunity to be intense and nostrilly; in an on-camera class at Stella Adler, I got to play an angry young farmer from *Spoon River Anthology* as well as characters from *Fargo* and *Living in Oblivion.* I dreamed of the day when I would be a celebrated performer and my erstwhile instructors could say, in the manner of a Midwestern piano teacher, "He took from me."

THE MORE TIME I spent in the presence of performers, the more time I found myself a rapt and sometimes appalled spec-tator to their self-promotional gambits. Be it other actors claw-ing for more *Godzilla* screen time, or teachers shilling some unique strain of sadopedagogy, everyone, it seemed, was a li-censed distributor of his own eponymous eponymousness.

I became more aware of it amongst nonperformers, too. For instance, I noticed that, in an apparent attempt to promote an agenda of self-interest, people—particularly older men—were wearing their pajamas in public. The phenomenon first came to my attention while I was reading *The New York Times:* Mafia don Vincent "the Chin" Gigante, I learned, had been repeatedly seen walking around his neighborhood wearing only his pajamas, a fact probably not unrelated to the widely held opinion that Gigante had been feigning mental illness in order to elude arrest by federal agents. As soon as I read this, I was reminded of *Duplex Planet,* a zine that consists of interviews with residents of nursing homes; in one issue, a resident is quoted as saying, "If you are an old man, and you go into a bar in pyjamas, people will buy you drinks."

On linking these two incidents in my mind, I experienced a vague sense of reassurance—after all, I have always imagined that I will spend my dotage in an emotional state that is best described as *unglued.* But then I came across two examples of young pajama wearers as well: one night at nine o'clock I saw a woman in her sleepwear walking down Seventh Avenue on the arm of an adoring male; a few days later I learned that Madonna had promoted her album *Bedtime Stories* by throwing a public pajama party at the club Webster Hall.

Presented, as I was, with an ever-widening portrait of pajama exploitation, I felt as if I were being excluded from some sort of cultural rite; I found myself identifying with the Mia Farrow character in *Rosemary's Baby.* Was I missing out on something? Was wearing pajamas in public a sign by which the powerful recognized one another? My unease was exacerbated by the fact that I do not wear pajamas, even within the confines of my own home, because they tend to entangle; I prefer sleeping in the altogether, gamboling and romping amidst the linens like a happy bedtime otter.

And so, eager to allay my troubled mind, I spent, over the course of a week, twenty hours wearing pajamas in public. First, of course, I had to buy some pajamas; I went to a local clothier and, ruling out any design revolving around teddy bears, ice cream, or professions thought glamorous by nine-year-olds, I opted for thin, vertical, dark green and red stripes. At home I suited up and looked at myself in my mirror; I looked not unlike a bar code.

My first forays were simple tasks—I went to a coffee bar, I went to the library. En route to this second destination, I walked through Washington Square Park, where my attire piqued the interest of a couple seated on a park bench. "Hey, Pajama Man!" the man greeted me. "You feeling too good for pants today?"

The woman next to him, presumably thinking I was an NYU student, asked, "Are you going to classes dressed like that?"

I replied, "No, I'm just not into a big clothing thing today," whereupon she gave me a thumbs-up sign. But then, when her friend started to avail me of his wares—"Smoke, smoke, buds"—I realized that the warm reception I had been given was nothing but a soft sell.

"If you're really going to do this," Jess had said of my new role, "You also have to wear slippers." And so, one cold and misty Saturday afternoon, I added to my sneakers and vertical stripes a hat and winter jacket and headed off for Bradlees at Union Square. Near the corner of Twelfth Street and Sixth Avenue I ran into my friend Michael. We greeted each other, then shared a slightly awkward pause. Then Michael, his voice betraying a note of embarrassment, said, "Can I ask you a strange question?"

I said sure.

"Are you, unh, are you wearing your pajamas?" I confirmed that I was. He said he hadn't recognized me in my getup. Then, perspicaciously, he asked if my attire had anything to do with Vincent Gigante; he also said that he had recently seen a woman walking around the Village at night wearing a bathrobe and nightgown. Michael's seizing of the trend was reassuring: I was not alone.

Once at Bradlees, I took off my hat and coat. My outfit drew many stares, including one from a young boy who identified me to his mother as a "sleep boat." Fearing that I had expressed a lack of originality in choosing striped pajamas, I asked a saleswoman for slippers shaped like either frogs or Pocahontas; she said neither were available in my size. "What I'd really like," I confessed, "are ones of the Indian in the Cupboard, but I don't think his movie was successful enough." The woman gazed at me in a manner suggesting that, whatever she was doing in the next thirty seconds, it would, in an ideal world, not involve me. I bought a pair of black quilted slip-ons.

At the World Financial Center I lingered near the counters of various food emporia, hoping for free samples; none were proffered. When a woman seated on a park bench in the Palm Court asked me why I was dressed the way I was, I told her, "I take my sleeping really seriously"; she smiled nervously and then looked down at the floor as if in search of a dog to pet. Later, a businessman walking side by side with another businessman said, "Hold on" to his companion, then took three steps out of his way to stare at me; I momentarily feared this was a fed who, thinking I was the *capo di tutti capi*, hoped to take me down in a spectacular atrium-based blood-fest.

I trundled over to Broad Street, where I got in line to take a tour of the New York Stock Exchange. "Are you from around here?" a young woman in line who had been eyeing me suspiciously asked.

"No," I said, "I'm from France." This sated her curiosity, and she went away.

When I reached the security-clearance area for the Exchange, the security guard said to me, "Sir, I'm going to ask you to step aside. I'm not sure they'll let you in like that, but I want

to check with a supervisor." I stepped aside; I was deeply grateful that I was not wearing Pocahontas slippers. The guard
walkie-talkied his supervisor, who appeared several minutes
later.

The broad-shouldered supervisor asked me, "Now, what's
going on here?"

The guard said, "That's him. I wasn't sure."

The supervisor winced slightly as he took in the pajamas,
and said, "No, we can't let you up like that." He invited me outside, where he asked me, "Are you feeling okay?" I said yes. He
asked why I had come to the Exchange.

I said, "Well, I'm interested in this line of work, but I'm not
sure I have the, unh, the *drive* for it."

He responded solemnly. "Look, put on a pair of dungarees,
a T-shirt, then come back. I'm not going to let you up like this."
I apologized and left.

I proceeded to Forty-second Street, where I visited several
porn-video stores. At one of these, I asked the burly, mustachioed manager, "Do you have any, unh, pajama videos?"

"Of men?" he asked.

"Of men, yeah," I said. "Or women. Either. But with, you
know, everyone in pajamas."

He walked toward the rear of the store, scanning the shelves.

"I had some lingerie ones," he said.

I asked, "Women in lingerie?"

He replied in the affirmative.

"I'm really just interested in the pajama ones, though," I
said.

He continued to browse the shelves for fifteen seconds or so
and concluded, "No, I don't think I have it." Eager to witness
examples of this pornographic subgenre, I went to three other
video stores and asked for pajama videos; alas, none of them
had ever heard of such a thing.

Were there such a thing, they would know about it at

Julius's. Julius's is a West Village gay bar frequented largely by older men—what is referred to as a "wrinkle room." Indeed, it was at Julius's that this pajama wearer felt best understood. "Why not?" one patron in his late sixties said to me when he had determined that I was, indeed, wearing pajamas and not a rented prison costume as he had thought. "I have days when I don't want to gussy up." And finally, I was rewarded at Julius's when a young Brooklynite named Tim bought me a drink. In fact, I was rewarded twice—for, some thirty minues later, as I was leaving, another patron—a gentleman of much warmth but not many teeth—flagged me down and, in a tone that bordered on the magisterial, said, "I think the pajamas are very sexy, and I hope they take you wherever you want to go tonight."

My days of pajama-wearing are behind me now. And, although I acknowledge that my earlier feelings of anxiety toward public pajama-wearing were unnecessarily vivid, I now realize that there is much to learn from this garment and its many applications. I was reminded that life is a question of context, and that it is highly influenced by the matter of location. One of the fears that accompanies growing old is the fear of becoming irrelevant; but swathed in a veritable snowstorm of paisleys or sea horses, you are, in the right location—say, the New York Stock Exchange—startlingly relevant.

I SUPPOSE IT was a foregone conclusion that, given my background as a humorist, the place where I would feel most relevant as a performer was in the trenches of comedy improvisation. During the next two years I would spend more than two hundred class-time hours studying this strange art, flourishing under the tutelage of teachers from Upright Citizens Brigade, Chicago City Limits, and ImprovOlympic. During the course of those two hundred or so hours, I would play an angry upstairs neighbor who threatens to throw uric acid on the neighbors below, a born-again Christian nudist, a devil worshipper who has been brought to meet his girlfriend's family for the first time and spends the whole evening crying, a Swedish farmer who is "pig-biting mad," a jilted bisexual who is "pig-biting mad," a sleepy air-traffic controller who is "pig-biting mad," the ambassador to Micronesia, God, Winona Ryder pretending to be Wynonna Judd, a voluble Asian man who is not embarrassed about sniffing the undersides of dogs, a surly biker, the color blue, a young Amish boy confused to learn that L.A. and Los Angeles are names for the same place, a town in Ohio that is jealous of Akron's success and thus has changed its name to Agron, an actress who is unsure if she is Karen Allen or Brooke Adams and thus has changed her name to Karen Adams, a truck driver at a diner who is writing a book called *Many Tiny, Invisible Dance Instructors Are Living Inside the Salt Shakers,* a whiny Native American actor who has started his own actors union called NAAG, a high school science teacher whose students have based his nickname on one of the periodic table's elements—Boring—and a young man in a cooking class who took a highly literal interpretation of a sugar-cookie recipe's direction to "roll in powdered sugar" and as a result is soon to be stung to death by bees.

I PERFORMED IMPROV four times for paying audiences—once in conjunction with a Chicago City Limits class and three times with fellow Upright Citizens Brigade students. With each successive performance I would become increasingly familiar with the physiology of terror: how swirly abdominal cramping is the bellwether to tingly, burning shoulder tension, which is the harbinger of arid-making esophageal constriction.

I tried to pour everything that I had heretofore learned into my work—not only the ability to be big and loud and slightly offensive, which I had learned from playing Oberon outdoors in London, and the inclination to turn feelings of disappointment (the Sills workshop) into gonzo abandon (*Godzilla*), but also the propensity for toughness that I had started to develop with Patterson, and the unembarrassment with which I had had to hurl my body across the studios of the Martha Graham School of Contemporary Dance.

The most important thing I have learned as an improviser is that a joke or bit that does not produce laughter is not a failure; it is only a failure if you don't send it over, if you don't, in the words of choreographers nationwide, "sell it." Conviction, or the illusion thereof, is all.

Would that this lesson had been an unnecessary one; would that my every utterance, my every literary effort had been a flawless, multifaceted gem. Alas, such is not the case. Three years ago, were I having a conversation with, say, an editor I would like to write for, or a person at a party that I would like to become friends with, and a witticism I proffered fell noticeably flat, I would be slightly shaken and would gradually recede from the conversation.

Now I just keep talking, but somewhat louder.

This is not what I would have expected from more than two hundred hours of comedy improv; I expected at the outset that improv would actually make me funnier as a person. But my conversation, two hundred hours later, is in no way any more sparkling or laugh-evoking as a result.

However, now you can hear every word of it.

The other way in which improvisation has informed my life is more philosophical. Both Upright Citizens Brigade and ImprovOlympic practice a form of improvisation that is called the Harold. In a Harold, only one suggestion is taken from the audience; this one suggestion sparks a monologue or series of monologues, which in turn spark three scenes, each of which are reprised three times. As the three scenes are reprised, their narratives start to overlap, turning the Harold (which usually lasts about a half hour) into a kind of play. The Harold was invented in the 1960s by comedy guru Del Close, who mentored Bill Murray, Gilda Radner, John Belushi, and John Candy when they were at Second City; it is also the teat of improvisation upon which younger pups like Mike Myers, Andy Dick, Andy Richter, and the members of the Upright Citizens Brigade suckled.

Doing a Harold necessitates a kind of groupthink. I remember once doing one at Solo Arts Theater, the theater where Upright Citizens Brigade performs, which was inspired by a monologue about abandonment. As the monologue had also touched upon the themes of theft and vision, I had a strong desire to play a blind person who accuses all sighted people of being "cornea felons." But when my colleagues' scenes started to unroll, strangely, someone else initiated a scene in which a blind older sister is mean-spiritedly saying of her blind younger sister, "She's not really blind—she just wants attention." So suddenly I had to change plans lest our Harold be peopled exclusively by irritable blind people. So instead I played a photographer who plagiarizes famous photographs.

Find the hole, fill the hole.

⸻

ONE HOLE IN my life, it seemed, was political commentary. Why did I so rarely turn my satirist's eye on the government? So when, one balmy morning, I saw a photograph in *The New York Times* of a New York Police Department badge, complete with a caption reading, "Citizens can rent a police officer for private functions," I became determined to use my improv skills to see if I might shed some light on this strange new development in law enforcement. After all, who among us, presented the opportunity to stanch the flow of irritations and small inequities posed us by the defenders of the law, would be so cavalier as to decline the invitation? Not I; coiled beneath my placid exterior lies the word *jackboot.*

The article explained that the Paid Detail Program, or Rent-a-Cop as it is known informally, costs twenty-seven dollars an hour, plus handling fees; the uniformed officer comes complete with a bulletproof vest and the power of arrest. Like most privatization schemes, the official rationale behind the program is to increase city services at minimal expense to the city; the unofficial rationale is to put more money in the pockets of police officers. The police department has tried, by vetting all potential renters and by rotating Paid Detail officers, to stem the possibility of officers forming divided loyalties, but there is little it can do to ameliorate the program's essential elitism—the affluent, after all, will get more protection.

While many have raised important, legitimate questions about the program—is it unfair that officers come not only indemnified by the city, but with equipment, training, and benefits provided by taxpayers? Will oversubscribed officers be less fit for regular duty? Has anyone seen *Robocop*?—my own questions have run more along the lines of "Can I exploit this recent development for my own highly personal ends?" Eager to find out, I walked over to my local precinct—the Sixth, on West Tenth. I told an officer standing behind the desk—a dark, burly man eating a cheeseburger—that I was interested in hiring an officer through the Paid Detail Program for one night several weeks hence.

"I'm having a party on my roof," I explained.

"A big one?" he asked.

"About ten people," I explained. "But there's a couple coming in from Philadelphia with their three-year-old, whom I've never met, and I just think that a uniformed officer would, unh, set a certain tone."

He lifted his right eyebrow skeptically.

"Yeah, I don't know," he said doubtfully.

Reaching down on the desk for a pen and a scrap of paper, he gave me a phone number to call, telling me to ask for Sergeant Murray. Back at home, I called the sergeant and re-asserted my needs. Sergeant Murray explained that it would not be possible because Paid Detail is available only to businesses, and a month's notice is required for vetting. However, he asked, "What kind of party is it?"

"Small—ten people," I said. "But I just think that, for some people, outdoors spells *crazy time.*"

"But it's on a roof. It's not like you're out in the open."

"Even still. Now, what kind of response time would we be looking at if the officer needed to radio in for backup?"

He explained that that information could only be given to vendors who had been vetted.

I decided to wait a few weeks and then call Sergeant Murray's office back with a second possible Paid Detail assignment. Because I had used my own voice the first time I called, I needed to disguise it the second time around lest Murray or any of his colleagues recognize me. Not wanting to use any accent that, in my nervousness, might slip away from me, I opted for a slightly New Yawk sound. The officer who answered the phone asked me to describe my event; I explained, "The co-op board I'm on is having a meeting about whether to put up storm windows." He wondered why I felt we needed police.

"The topic of storm windows unleashes a lot of crabbiness amongst the tenants," I explained, "and I just think that a uniformed officer would cut the Crab Factor right in half." He calmly told me that most Paid Detail assignments are related to "security, peddler situations, chronic traffic problems."

"I was also wondering," I said, "who defines the terms of arrest. Does an officer on Paid Detail have to uphold state and federal laws? Our assistant secretary is often late to meetings, and I just think that a little law enforcement might send the message home."

"An off-duty officer is bound by the same rules and regulations that an on-duty one is," he said matter-of-factly. "We're not there to adjudicate little internal problems, nor to be a proctor. As long as no one gets hit—that's all I care about."

He paused, then concluded, "I don't think a Paid Detail situation is what you're looking for." He suggested that, if violence erupted, I alert an on-duty officer.

Several days later I called the Paid Detail office with yet a third scenario. This being the third time that I had called, I felt slightly nervous and decided that, in addition to a new voice— a breathy, very emphatic, Southern voice—I should think a little about my character and his proclivities. Sitting down at my desk with a notepad, I jotted down a short list—"Truman Capote. Heavy cologne use. Slightly frantic. Moved to New York last year. Candied violets. Owns, and resembles, a small, shivery dog." I picked up the phone and called the Paid Detail office.

"I'm decorating an apartment on Park Avenue," I told the officer who answered the phone, "and my client has hired, without my permission, an additional decorator. So there'll be three days in October where he and I'll be working side by side. I don't know if you've ever had the experience of being in the same room as two members of the design community; I will simply evoke the phrase *tears before bedtime*."

The officer took my name and number, saying someone would call me back. No one did.

After I waited for several weeks, it gradually dawned on me that it was unwise to look to my city for adjudication and the means of retribution. When justice entered my life, I now realized, it would not take the form of a gun-toting individual exhibiting a predilection for the phrase *Move along, bub.* No, the message was clear: it was every man for himself.

•

THE POLICE DEPARTMENT had shown little or no interest in my desire to arrest others.

Now I had to see if *I* could get arrested.

Two

GINGERLY, I STARTED to audition. Reading *Backstage* (and later its Los Angeles counterpart, *Drama-Logue*) each week, I was struck by two things: first, these two trade papers are like catalogues of desperation; second, all student films being made at New York University are about "isolation of the conscience."

On the former front there was a wealth of evidence. "MALES: age 17–22, white, fair-complexioned. Experience of family members's death useful," read a casting notice for one television project; another notice ran, "A SMALL DOG: who can perform tricks on command. However, all types and ages will be considered. Children are welcome." A character description for a low-budget film went yet further: "ALEX: 20's, attractive, witty, with great comedic timing and improv skills, must be able to speak with English and Indian (cabdriver) accents, some knowledge of Hebrew and Spanish a plus, needs to blow smoke rings, have knowledge of guitar, with apartment for a two- to three-day shoot (ideally a one or more bedroom with a long hallway, living area, and fire escape/balcony that gets great sunrises)." The notices for women, unsurprisingly, dwelled on physical characteristics: "LINDA: gorgeous girl, beautiful face,

blonde; ALLISON: the same as Linda but with black or red hair";
a "loving couple with full hearts but empty arms" took out a
classified ad in *Backstage* for an egg donor, stating, "Ideal candi-
date will look like Nastassja Kinski."

Having majored in film at New York University, I was, of
course, particularly interested in reading about what kinds of
films were being made there now. During my college days in
the early eighties, the totemic influence over most of the film
students was NYU graduate Martin Scorsese (Woody Allen, we
all knew, had been expelled from NYU when, on a metaphysics
exam, he was caught looking into the soul of the boy sitting
next to him); the vast majority of us, it seemed, wanted to make
edgy, realistic movies with strong personal statements. We did
not want to make glossy, childlike movies in which adorable
aliens from the sky learned to enjoy and disseminate snack
foods. That was Hollywood. We were New York. But now, thirteen years later, looking through *Backstage* at the casting notices for NYU films, the somewhat dark-hued tenor of my
generation's cinematic aspirations had grown yet darker and
had crossed over into the truly grim—over a twelve-month period I encountered notices not only for the aforementioned
film about "isolation of the conscience," but also for "*Death of a
Broken Heart,* a silent film inspired by German Expressionism";
a senior thesis called *Asylums of the Soul,* "an urban fairy tale
involving invisible birds, severed limbs, and abject loneliness";
and "*Pain of Truth,* about a person on the brink of suicide." I
felt old. But unburdened.

Auditioning does not produce the dread and nausea in me
that it does in others. Auditioning gets a bad name because it is
highly time-consuming and because it is not an accurate gauge
of everyone's talent. I like to think of an audition as a very, very
short run of a play: I rehearse, I open, I get pulverized by critics, I weep over a quantity of gin, I go home stronger. To be

sure, having auditioned many actors in the past is a boon to me in the present. I have learned from others' mistakes—I now know *not* to lick the casting person's hand, even if it is an interesting way to illustrate how a devil-worshipping cult member in a Sylvester Stallone film might try to ensnare her victim; I also know *not* to start out an audition by dropping the bombshell "Ray Stark is my cousin."

On the To Do side of the spectrum, I suppose that the most important discovery I have made is one related to memorization. No casting director expects an actor to have memorized the dialogue he's reading. However, the more familiar the actor is with the material, the more eye contact he can engage in with the casting director or reader. This eye contact is of especial importance at the beginning, the climax, and the end of the scene. The actor who has memorized these three parts of the scene can thus assert his eerily powerful presence at the most important points in the audition and can thus create a small pageant of affect whose individual components might be labeled First Impressions, Tender Moment, and Parting Glances—each a peak or valley in the topography of the audition, each a suitable name for a line of bathroom tissue.

I GOT A callback on the second thing I auditioned for. I had read about the show—Theaterworks' production of *Charlotte's Web*, which would tour nationally and be done in New York at the Promenade, a prestigious off-Broadway venue—in *Backstage*. Upon arriving at the large, raw rehearsal space in the garment district filled with more than eighty auditioners, I approached a table behind which sat two young, short-haired male monitors. When one of these monitors asked, "Do you know what you want to read for?" I explained that I wanted to read for Wilbur, the pig.

"Wilbur?" one of the young men asked indifferently.

"Yeah. Do you have to be fat for that?" I asked.

"No."

"Because I can do fat."

"Okay."

"I have fat in me."

Once poised inside the room where the director and his two colleagues sat in judgment, I got halfway through the scene—a plaintive one in which the little porker says, "I'm very young and have no real friends in the barn," then asks all the other animals if they'll be his friend, only to be told no—when the director stopped me and told me to go back outside and look at Homer, the farmer, instead. Twelve minutes later, feverishly running through the Homer scene while standing in line behind eight other actors, it was with some surprise that I heard a voice from the inner sanctum call out, "Henry! We want to see Henry now!" So I proceeded past the eight other actors—I *loved* this—and reentered the room.

Of the qualities that I have been led to believe I can play passably, dim-witted reigns supreme. So, harnessing my powers of aw-shucks naïveté, and blanketing these powers with an accent evocative of the bayou, this Homer grew excited at the sight of a spiderweb spelling TERRIFIC and then badgered my wife, Edith, into calling the newspapers. This went fairly swimmingly: laughs were laughed and compliments paid. But when, three days later, I returned for my callback and read the scene again, a cold, arctic wind seemed to rush through the room; I was a German shepherd who had been tied to a chain-link fence behind a Juneau, Alaska, outpost, and now I was hoarse from barking.

I auditioned for a production of Molière's *The Misanthrope*: No, thank you. A mockumentary about a male Rockette: No, thank you. An evening of Chekhov one-acts: We'll be in touch.

An independent feature about a bike messenger turned drug warlord: Please go away.

I thought I stood a chance with a nude *Measure for Measure* being done in the East Village. Not *all* the roles required nudity, just some, but to say that you were unwilling to shed clothing was to limit the number of roles for which you might be considered. The production was also to feature men in some of the women's roles and vice versa. Standing alone (and fully clothed) on the hazily lit, litter-strewn stage of a theater on East Fourth Street, I launched into my *Titus Andronicus* monologue, only to have the director cut me off midway with a disinterested "Henry, Henry, Henry. I'm going to bring you back. Look at Mariana, who's married to Angelo/Angela."

Out in the lobby I approached the monitor—a witty woman in her early thirties who had put a notice reading DO NOT BULLYRAGE, CAJOLE, OR DISCOUNTENANCE on the door—and asked her about Mariana. "How nude is that one? What's the johnson factor on that role?"

"It's not frontal," she assured me. "It's backal. It'll probably be a toga drape, or maybe they'll go the classy Kevin Kline route with very tight tights."

"Sort of a 'package' effect."

"I haven't heard it put that way, but yes."

"But it won't be a big illuminated arrow pointed at my groin."

"Or if it is, everyone will know it's a joke."

"Okay, just wanted to check."

I never heard back from them.

On several occasions directors asked if I was interested in playing a very small role, say, something with one or two lines. I thought about this, then deemed myself far too grand. The artistic director of the Grove Street Playhouse, having seen me read for *The Three Bears' First Hanukkah,* which I thought was sort of funny, wanted me to read instead for a treacly Hans Christian Andersen adaptation called *Santa and the Snow Queen*. The role was a winsome grandson; I only needed to read one scene to see it all before me—a nightshirt and rosy cheeks, and lots of dialogue like, "Let us go then, Mother, to seek winter's snowy mantle."

"I'm really only interested in the Hanukkah play," I told the artistic director. She looked at me questioningly. I explained, "This one is sort of sweet. The Hanukkah one has a little *grit*."

As soon as I said *grit*, her eyes widened, and it was clear that my comment had not endeared me to her. Several minutes later, in the theater's lobby, one of the other actors—a stocky, unshaven guy in his late thirties—caught my eye and, chuckling, mimicked, "Grit." He added, "What were you expecting, *The Godfather*?"

THE STRANGEST (AND LONGEST) audition I have gone on was one for *Noah* and *Behold the Lamb*, two biblical epics to be performed by hundreds of actors in an enormous, two-thousand-seat theater outfitted with a three-hundred-foot wraparound stage, in Strasburg, Pennsylvania. Having called a phone number in *Backstage*, I received an application from the shows' producing organization, Sight and Sound Theaters. One million audience members, a letter of introduction explained, would attend the 784 performances of *Noah* and *Behold the Lamb* in 1999 alone. I also learned that seventy-five live animals and more than two hundred animatronic ones would help the audience of *Noah* experience "the feeling of actually 'being inside the ark.'" Meanwhile, *Behold the Lamb* "presents one of the most dramatic onstage portrayals of the life of Jesus Christ ever produced for live theater. The show spans from Christ's baptism at the age of thirty, to his ministry, death, victorious resurrection, and concludes with his heavenly reign. Special effects will include pyro, fog, laser, and media."

Also enclosed was a Spiritual Life Questionnaire. My own religious beliefs leaning, in a highly disorganized way, toward agnosticism, I do not have a particularly vivid relationship with Jesus and thus was hard-pressed to come up with a compelling answer to the questionnaire's instruction "Describe your personal relationship with Jesus Christ." I finally came up with "Christ is an icon of selflessness and charity. All people—but especially actors—could profit from his example." The questionnaire also asked, "Will you allow your 'Christlikeness' to lead and guide you if employed at Sight and Sound? How would you do this?" I responded, "By making charitable comments to other performers and theater artists. Running lines with others. Working the box office. Helping with pyro. Utilizing goat skills."

I drove down to Strasburg the morning of my audition. That the Millennium Theater is a sprawling, fountain-bedecked monstrosity is made all the stranger by the fact that it and its satellite, the Living Waters Theater, are located in the heart of Amish country. In my mind's eye I saw an Amish barn-raising: as the side of the barn is hoisted skyward, a lone tuft of marabou plumage, dislodged from last year's Mary Magdalene costume and now airborne, gently drifts down, landing on an eighteenth-century farm implement.

Twenty-three of us had assembled in folding metal chairs in the Living Waters, each prepared to sing thirty-two bars and do a one-minute monologue. A friendly, balding director in his forties greeted us once we were all seated, then led us in prayer.

"We hope you're honored by our being here today," the director prayed. "You already know who should be in the show and who should not."

Once spread out on the eighty-foot stage, all twenty-three

of us were taught a forty-second dance routine in which we were meant to emanate "awe and wonderment." The routine was slowish, and thus seemingly easy, yet when I was asked to perform it with a group of three other men for the director and choreographer's inspection, I managed to bump into one of my fellow dancers, a blond fellow in a Mickey Mouse T-shirt, who shot me a glance that was distinctly un-Christlike.

Back out in the lobby, I waited an hour to sing my song ("Hey, Jude") and do my *Spoon River* monologue. When my conversation with several other auditioners turned to the topic of how deceptively difficult the dance routine had been, the fellow I had bumped into during the dance routine asked me, "Was that hard for you?" whereupon, suddenly feeling as if I needed to generate an excuse, I blurted, "I grew up in a Seventh-Day Adventist household, so: not a lot of singing and dancing in my background."

After I had done my song and monologue, three other auditioners and I were, surprisingly, taken upstairs for a special assignment—another dance routine. In this one, we were Noah's family, who, upon seeing that the forty days of rain have subsided, launch into a frenzy of precision choreography. This routine—likened by the choreographer to that most unlikely event, an "Amish hoedown"—was far more complex than the first. I memorized it thusly: Skip 2-3, kick back, kick back, Artful Dodger right, Artful Dodger left, pivot 2-3-4, jumping jack, jumping jack, littlekickleft, littlekickright, spin-bam! spin-bam!, pivot 2-3-4, polka downstage, polka upstage, polka down, polka up, big spin-bam!

"Wow," one of the other dancers said to the choreographer after two of us had mentioned that all the spinning was making us dizzy, "and we would be doing this whole thing while body miked?"

"Yeah, the whole show is body miked," the choreographer

said. "Except for the Via Dolorosa. You can't mike Christ on the cross."

No, no, no, we all murmured, all empathy and feigned understanding, you wouldn't put a mike on a crucified man.

Down in the lobby again, we waited about an hour to perform our routine. When one of the other dancers told me that she, too, was from New York City, I asked her, "What will you do if you're cast in the show?"

"I'll say, 'Thank you, Jesus!' "

I botched the dance routine fairly badly, unable to pull off any of the spins. Slightly sweaty, and with heart hammering from the exertion, I walked back to the lobby to complete the last part of my audition—a "spiritual talk" with the theater's pastor. The pastor, a kindly, skinny, fortysomething gentleman accompanied by his kindly, skinny, fortysomething wife, had been sitting hard by the copy machine in the theater's utility closet, conducting one-on-one talks with each auditioner.

"Please excuse my flushed state," I told the pastor, "I'm just coming out of a very difficult dance routine."

"Oh, no problem," he said, offering to wait a few minutes if needed. I assured him I was fine.

The three of us talked for twelve minutes, covering topics ranging from what it means to be a Christian to my own development as one. When the pastor asked me if I considered myself "reborn," I said, "I'm uncomfortable with that term." Doesn't it imply that, prior to rebirth, I was dead? No, no, the pastor assured me—you don't have to be dead to be spiritually awakened. Okay, I assented. I guess I'm reborn.

"We have certain lifestyle guidelines that we want to talk to you about," the pastor said, explaining that, in the "God-honoring" world of Sight and Sound, drinking, smoking, and sex, "whether it's male-female or female-female," were not tolerated. I wasn't sure what aspect of my person had prompted him to warn me against engaging in lesbian sex. But I thought it wise to mention, "I have a boyfriend."

"Mm-hmm."

"But he probably wouldn't be around during the run of the show."

"Okay, well, that would, that would fit within our guidelines."

"Good."

"Now, do you have any questions for us?"

"Would there be snakes in the show?" I am deathly afraid of snakes.

"Snakes?" the pastor asked uncertainly.

"I just wonder if there isn't a, unh, Pentecostal element to the show."

The pastor looked at his wife. He looked at the side of the copy machine. Then he looked at me and asked, "What do you mean?"

"I was thinking of the Pentecosts who do snake-handling."

"That's a radical strain of Pentecostalism," he told me. "There are many Pentecosts who don't handle snakes."

"Oh, okay. I just wondered because, unh, I won't work with snakes."

The pastor asked his wife, "Are there snakes on the ark?"

"That's a good question," she said, genuinely curious. "I'm not sure. We should find out."

We talked for a few more minutes, and then I drove home. During the drive, I started to daydream about what kind of role I might be asked to play in a Sight and Sound production. I envisioned the following. A pin spot isolates me downstage left— I am in a diaper, sprawled in a wicker basket that is floating amidst a thicket of bulrushes. But as more lights come up, we gradually reveal that I am not alone—in fact, there are ninety of us in diapers, each sprawled in his own wicker basket floating amidst a thicket of bulrushes. The lights achieve a blinding intensity as a chorus of angelic voices bursts out: *Everything's Coming Up Moses.*

"WHAT HAPPENED WITH those Bible shows?" Jess asked me six weeks later.

I explained that the shows' organizers had sent me a letter saying I was wait-listed but then had never gotten in touch again.

"I guess God is saving me for a higher purpose," I said.

Jess offered an unconvincing "Unh-huh."

"Plus," I added, "those are both big snake shows."

"Oh?"

"Absolutely. Both shows: drenched in snake."

9 ALSO TRIED TO peddle my thespian wares at Actors Connection, an outfit where actors pay to be seen by agents
and casting people. These sessions always started with a member of the Actors Connection dispensing recent talent-industry
news to the twenty or so actors in attendance; as it has been ten
years since I worked in casting, none of the names that were
dropped meant anything to me, and sounded made-up.

"Stacey Powderbottom is casting regional theater now for
the Slash Group," a typical bulletin would run. All the actors in
the room, formerly jangly and dissipated in their energies,
would snap to attention at the mention of Stacey Powderbottom's name.

"Perpetua VandelGrub has gone over to Jack Flankfist's office." Astonished looks all around; "Wasn't Perpetua here last
week?" the looks seemed to say. "The one with the Rice Krispies
spilled all down her front?"

"Don Trunk is now an *associate* casting director at Vile and
Vile." Looks of encouragement all around; we always knew Don
Trunk had it in him; Don Trunk is a *doll*.

"And the commercial department at Framer and Trap will
now be run by Tina Buttons." Looks of mild irritation—Tina

Buttons never calls anyone from Actors Connection; Tina Buttons just comes to pick up a paycheck; Tina Buttons should get off the grift.

The guest would then be introduced, and each person in the session would have the opportunity either to do a monologue or scene or to read copy.

I attended five of these sessions, to no avail. Lynne Jebens of the Krasny office said to my scene partner and me, "Guys, what did I just tell the last two people? *Pacing.* That was soooo slow and dragged-out. It should be like two cats circling their prey. People, I'll say it again, Pacing, pacing, pacing!" An agent named Bill Schill encouraged me to get new pictures. Casting director Alycia Aumuller told me, "A comedy background is very marketable"; her colleague Tracey Goldblum from the Abrams agency told me I reminded her of Greg Kinnear. And when I had finished doing a cereal commercial for David Coakley of J. Michael Bloom, he shouted warmly, "Bill Irwin speaks!"

I followed up with the last three parties, sending thank-you notes and a copy of my book to their offices. None called back.

CHAPTER 10

*U*NDER THE FROTHY surf of the charitable act lies an ocean of murk.

I had tried, throughout my young career as an aspiring performer, to avoid getting help from friends, lest I incur complication and heartbreak. But when Martin, a friend since high school, offered some help, I decided to bite. In retrospect, not a brilliant decision on my part.

Martin was writing a magazine profile of a woman I'll call Rachel, the producer of a hip TV show that often featured the work of comics and performers whose sensibilities are not dissimilar from my own. Over the course of two weeks, Martin had been telling me how much he was enjoying interviewing Rachel. He had not yet met her face-to-face—he had been interviewing her over the phone—but she had already proven to be charming, funny, sharp. And sexy? You'd have to be insensate not to pick up on the erotic tinge to Martin's bulletins from the journalistic front.

Rachel, Martin reported, knew and liked my writing. He rightly thought that she and I might like to meet each other. Rachel was flying in from Los Angeles that Friday; she and Martin would have a drink that night, maybe off the record, maybe on; then Martin would call me Saturday to arrange a time for Rachel and me to meet. It looked like she was going to be downtown in the West Village, where I live; maybe she and I could go to Clementine for a drink.

Was Martin—a talented journalist less established than me—hoping that, by helping me out, I would in turn recommend him to some of my editors? Was Martin trying to impress Rachel by introducing her to his obscure but promising humorist friend? These questions only come to me in retrospect; at the time, the planned meeting seemed like a situation in which everybody would win.

Martin called Saturday.

"So, was it . . . fraught?" I asked.

Rachel, it turned out, had been accompanied by two executives from the network, who had taken her out to dinner after the drink with Martin.

"I don't know," Martin said. "It was strange. But she's really a fascinating lady."

"Well, it sounds like maybe you two should be alone tomorrow," I said. "I feel a little . . ."

"No, no, don't be silly. She really wants to meet you."

He said he would call Sunday morning to tell me when and where to convene.

Indeed, he called the next day at eleven. He sounded slightly frantic. "She's having lunch at the Waldorf, and then she has to be at NBC at two o'clock. Why don't you come to the bar at one-fifteen?"

As soon as he said "one-fifteen," my mind flashed to the scene in *The Prime of Miss Jean Brodie* wherein Maggie Smith, summoned to the headmistress's office at three-fifteen, says, "She thinks to intimidate by the use of the quarter hour." Maybe *intimidate* wasn't the right word to describe Martin's M.O., but I had the distinct impression that, were I to arrive at the bar between one and one-fourteen, my face would be the target area of a hard jet of civet.

Thinking that I should wait until Rachel was in town another time, or should simply talk to her on the phone sometime, I launched into a conversational wiggle. But Martin was in a rush.

"I don't know what the vibe's going to be," he said. "But be more effusive than you usually are so I don't get nervous."

This statement caused my cheeks to flush, either from embarrassment or anger, I wasn't sure. Impulsively, I blurted out, "If I don't show up, I'll leave a message on your machine."

"Fine. And I'll tell Rachel that you'll meet her as soon as the show's ratings are better."

"*What?*"

"I'm kidding! Jesus, don't be so weird, Hank . . ."

Angered, I stomped around my apartment for an hour, wondering if I should bother going. I vehemently scrubbed a dirty saucepan; I committed a small act of violence on a misshapen salad fork. Clearly, irritability exuded from me like a powerful musk; was meeting a potential employer in this state a wise move? Moreover, it was raining. It was one thing to arrive angry, and another to arrive *wet* and angry. No. Remain.

Ten minutes later: yes. Go. Rachel is the preeminent purveyor of hip, slightly jaundiced comedy, and if I don't show up, I am putting out a fire, I am closing a door, I am burning a bridge, I am committing hundreds of wood-based metaphors evocative of career death. Yes.

I trudged to the subway with the alacrity of an arthritic donkey. Arriving at the bar at the appointed quarter hour, I detected no sign of Martin or Rachel. I walked back to the lobby and looked there. Then back to the bar. Back to the lobby. Back to the bar.

I walked outside. The rain had subsided. I found a pay

phone on Forty-second Street and left a bewildered message on Martin's answering machine. As soon as I hung up the phone, I started to cry—here I was yet again, failed and inappropriate. It was as if there were a placard hanging over my head that read FAVORITE BEATLE: RINGO. Had I screwed up? Had I been jilted? Why was my career so middling? Why do so many of my efforts meet with blankness or silence? Do others perceive my cautiousness as hostility? I felt like my foray into the performing arts had caused me to exceed my bite/chew ratio.

I took the subway home. The next day Martin faxed me a note suggesting I send Rachel a copy of my book. He included her address in Los Angeles.

I seized the phone and called him.

"What happened?" I asked. "Did things get hubba hubba or did you not go to the Waldorf?"

"What do you mean?"

"I went and you weren't there. Didn't you get my message?"

He ignored this question, saying simply that he and Rachel had been sitting at the bar.

"Really? Because I looked a couple of times and you weren't there."

He calmly reiterated that they had been sitting at the bar.

"Rachel *did* get up to use the bathroom at one point. I might have gotten up at the same time, too. I can't remember."

You had sex in the bathroom of the Waldorf? I wanted to blurt out, but thought better.

I expressed my anxiety that Rachel would think I had stood her up; Martin assured me that he had told her he wasn't sure I could come in the first place.

When I hung up the phone I realized that I was of two minds. As Martin's *friend,* I hoped that he and Rachel had had an assignation. They were both single, attractive people who clearly liked each other—why *not* turn a hotel bathroom stall into a torrid, Lysol-redolent stand-up sex chamber? Many have done so.

As Martin's *colleague,* however, I felt differently. As Martin's *colleague,* I thought, yes, why not turn a hotel bathroom stall into a torrid, Lysol-redolent stand-up sex chamber, but why not do it in such a manner that others are not simultaneously paging you in the lobby? The experience is marred.

What was disquieting to me, though, was that Martin and I were close enough, and Martin was candid enough, that he would have had no qualms confiding to me if indeed the tide of events had turned erotic. So why the smoke screen? Maybe Rachel, in an act of gossip containment, asked Martin not to say anything lest her reputation undergo besmirchment. After all, you aren't supposed to sleep with the journalist who is profiling you—it is overly hospitable and may injure the winsome quality of the writer's prose.

Or maybe the fault was mine. Maybe they *had* both gone to the bathroom for nonsexual ends.

Of course, this last scenario was the one that my mind fastened onto and proceeded to work over and over, like a six-year-old with his scabby knee. In this scenario I was once again the loser; I was the man with the impulse but not the follow-through; I was pointing the loaded gun, but the only target I could hit was my own foot.

IT WAS AT this point that I devoted my energies to convincing delicatessens and dry cleaners to hang up my head shot. It seemed the logical course of action.

CHAPTER 11

THE SHOPPER WALKING in my direction, a weary-looking woman in her late forties, was staring at the beautiful, star-shaped bottle I was holding in my right hand.

"Would you like to try a fragrance made with chocolate?" I asked in my most sincere manner. She gazed at me dubiously but slowed to a stop.

"This is Angel," I said, referring to the bottle. "It's made without florals. It's Thierry Mugler's new fragrance."

She took the scent card that I handed her and proceeded to sniff it.

"It's made with fruit as its top notes," I continued. "Its midnotes are chocolate, caramel, honey, and vanilla."

That I had just described what appeared to be the makings of an elaborate sundae seemed to hang in the air between us.

"So now you can have your chocolate with or without calories," I added, as I had been instructed to.

The woman stared at me with a curious expression—part indulgence, part incredulity, part rebuke. Embarrassed, I looked down at the floor. Seconds later, when I looked up again, she was still standing and staring.

It was then that I recognized her expression: it was the look that a mother gives her wayward son.

....

DURING THE AFTERNOON that I spent spraying and selling fragrance on the mezzanine of Saks Fifth Avenue's flagship Fifth Avenue store, I learned many things. I learned how to pronounce *ylang-ylang* ("ee-LANG-ee-LANG"). I learned that, while some women want to be swept up by the romance and imagery peculiar to fragrance—flying unicorns using their spiraled horns to pierce gauzy, aroma-laden rainbows; members of several generations of a family in Grasse shaking off their pastis hangovers in order to handpick jasmine blossoms at dawn—most women simply want to make a surgical strike on the Lancôme counter. And I learned more than I ever knew—indeed, more than I ever thought was possible to know—about the highly fascinating fragrance-application process known as *layering*.

Now, I grant you, this was no *Peer Gynt*. Selling perfume is to acting as subscribing to the Fruit-of-the-Month Club is to farming. And yet, having now devoted a sizable chunk of my life to developing my acting skills, I was overcome by a need to apply these skills in the workplace. Any workplace.

....

WHEN YOU USE the employee entrance to enter Saks's first floor, you walk up a gently inclined ramp that is emblazoned, in two sets of increasingly larger type, "smile, smile, SMILE, SMILE; smile, smile, SMILE, SMILE." This became my byword.

I apprised myself of a variety of fragrances' compositions and qualities—or, as is said in the exalted language of the world of fragrance, of a variety of fragrances' "product stories." From a handbook given to purveyors of Ralph Lauren's Safari, for instance, I learned that the Safari wearer "enjoys a life of freedom and movement bred by the heritage and confidence of old world stature"; its accompanying bath and body line has a "strong product story built around [its] active ingredient . . . macadamia nut oil." There are two key plot points to the story that is macadamia-nut oil. One is that the nut's strength comes from having withstood environmental elements, the other is that the nut's softness comes from its high percentage of moisture. Granted, not the stuff of high drama—there is no reason to believe that macadamia-nut oil will be coming soon to a theater near you—but the fact that Safari is the only fragranced bath and body line to contain macadamia-nut oil makes Safari unique and gives salespeople something to talk about.

And so, minutes later, as I handed out scent cards for Laura Biagotti's fragrance Venezia ("ven-ETS-ee-ah"), I would remind customers that *Venezia* was the Italian word for Venice and that Miss Biagotti was a designer well known for her sunglasses; as I handed out samples of Angel, I would tell customers that Thierry Mugler smelled more than six hundred fragrances before choosing Angel and that the fragrance's star-shaped bottles were so intriguing that Saks customers had been stealing them. And, of course, at the behest of the counter supervisors I was working for, I would remind all customers, regardless of their interest in the topic, that the best way to make a fragrance last longer is to buy that fragrance's accompanying lotion and then *layer* the two.

Indeed, chief among the challenges of the fragrance sprayer is engaging the interest of potential customers. Consider, for instance, the following interaction: "Are you looking for a Valentine's Day gift?" I asked one shopper, thinking that I was posing a question fraught with possibility.

"I'm Brazilian," she said, and fled.

Similarly: "Are you interested in trying a fragrance made with chocolate?" I asked another shopper.

"No."

A SALESWOMAN NAMED Krista and I joined forces in an attempt to get two scruffy girls in their early twenties who had stopped in front of us to buy Angel. I had been having little success luring customers with the adorable utterance "From one Angel to another" and was glad to try a little teamwork; somehow the quality that this salesman needed to muster—the aforementioned conviction, or the illusion thereof—seemed more readily available when I was cast as a foil.

Krista and I, both standing in front of the Angel counter and both holding sprayed scent cards, spun a fine web of enticement for the two girls: the fragrance was new, was from Paris, had been chosen over six hundred others, was alluring to guys like me (I nodded my head copiously during this portion of the sales pitch), was made with chocolate, was not tainted by heinous elements like lily of the valley or freesia, and came in a fabulous and often-stolen bottle. The girls listened enthusiastically—Paris! Guys! Chocolate!—but as we got more and more specific about sizes and prices, they became increasingly giggly until, finally, one of them said, "Okay? I really have to go to the bathroom?" and that was that. ("They'll be back," Krista told me when they had flitted off. "They have to digest it. It's very futuristic, it's very *Star Wars*.")

Closing a sale was not easy. After my fair-to-middling performance with Krista and Angel, "the fragrance of the future," it was time to take my act on the road. My vehicle was to be Issey Miyake ("ISS-see me-AH-kee"), a delicate, sparkle-clean white floral that is exclusive to Saks. Stationed at an Issey outpost on the outskirts of the main fragrance-traffic area—I was, theatrically speaking, opening in New Haven—I managed, within forty minutes, to send three customers over to the counter, one who bought 3.4 ounces (sixty-six dollars).

However, concurrent with my auspicious Issey stint was my

formation of this troubling question: Do customers ever really listen to or care what salespeople tell them? Especially in the heady world of fragrance, where blather is the coin of the realm, where everything is described as being "sophisticated" and "surprising" and "extravagant" and "knowing"? In an attempt to shine light on this question, I decided that, in my conversations with customers, I would . . . embellish the Issey product story. After one woman had allowed me to spray her wrist, I told her, "It's got sort of a warm, *buttery* quality." (Her response: "And what's it called? Do you have a little card?") When another woman I had sprayed said, "That smells good," I told her, "Yes, it's got sort of a warm *buttery smell*." (Her response: "How much is it?") With a third woman, I took a slightly different tack.

"Do you wear fragrance normally?" I asked after she had allowed me to spray her.

"I do, but I have to be very careful because some are too heavy and give me migraines. . . . It's obviously a base note in them."

"This base note has a little spice," I said of my product, "but it's very, very subtle."

"Right."

"The top note is lily of the valley, which is very light. It's refreshing. And it won't leave a residue like other perfumes." (She looked down at her wrist and said, "I think I'll let that waft off"; it was unclear whether she meant my sample or my comment.)

I HAD SPRAYED Issey, I had handed out Angel and Venezia, but I had still not experienced firsthand the thrill of the sell. And the sell, I knew, was all-important—when you work in retail, your goal is to elicit not warm, glowing prose from the man from the *Times,* but, rather, the dulcet tones of the cash register's ka-*ching!*

So I made my way over to the elegant, ivy-leaves-spray-painted-gold splendor of Annick Goutal ("ahh-NEEK goo-TAHL"), a French perfumer with a line of fourteen fragrances. Positioning myself behind the elaborately decorated Annick Goutal counter, I met with Claudia, the line's personable director of training, and David, the conscientious counter manager. David and Claudia apprised me of what would be the most complex and interesting product story I would encounter: first, the fragrance is a "wardrobe concept," meaning that the scents only last for a couple of hours, so users are encouraged to change or reapply scent as they change their clothes (buzz phrase: *from the boardroom to the bedroom*). This concept harkens back to the pre–Civil War period when women, using scents that were without chemicals and thus did not last long, were in the habit of reapplying their fragrance several times a day. Second, each fragrance is an "inspiration," meaning that, not only was each created by Annick Goutal to capture specific rapturous moments in her life—an especially beautiful twilight she once experienced, an especially beautiful beach she found on the island of Re—but that when customers apply the scents, they will be flooded with rapture.

"When they buy a fragrance," Claudia said, "they go home and it brings memories to them."

"Their own memories—or of Annick's beach vacation?" I asked.

"Whenever you wear one of these fragrances," Claudia told me, "it creates something in you. I have more women come up and say, 'Oh, my God, that reminds me of a time I had an affair.' "

The one fragrance in the line that would seem to be an exception to the inspiration concept is the citrussy *eau de toilette,* Eau d'Hadrien ("oh dah-dree-ENN")—a unisex fragrance named after the bisexual Roman emperor Hadrian. (Yes, Claudia reported, she *does* tell some customers that the fragrance is named after a bisexual. She herself sometimes wears Hadrien, she told me—"It helps me to balance my male and female animals.")

About twenty minutes after Claudia and David had briefed me, a woman in her late forties came up to the counter looking for a Valentine's Day gift for her mother. Casting a glance at David and Claudia, I sensed that the three of us might be able to induce this woman to buy, buy, buy—we were Mephistopheles and Gretchen and Valentin, and she was our Faust; we were the Three Weird Sisters, and she our Macbeth.

When I asked her if she wanted to try some Hadrien, she declined because she was already wearing Chanel No. 5; I rued a missed opportunity to balance her animals.

"My mother loves lily of the valley," the customer said.

David, Claudia, and I showed her some fragrances and discussed prices. (It is not unusual, they told me later, for the two of them to wait on one customer.) The woman seemed unsure of what to buy. I explained about the "inspirations," saying, "For instance, there's one fragrance called Sables, which means 'sand' in French—she was on the beach when she decided to create it; another is called Heure Exquise, which means 'exquisite hour' in French, that's that sort of twilight when day turns into night."

"Nice time of day," she said, warming to my conversational bait.

She looked over the fourteen fragrances, picking up bottles, smelling caps, dawdling. She expressed interest in lotion; David applied some on her.

"Another nice thing about the lotion," I began to natter on, "is that they advocate layering, so the idea is if you—"

She cut me off, apologizing for the state of her "dishwater hands."

"No, it's perfect for you, then," David argued.

"All the more reason to get it," I added.

But she couldn't make up her mind. I brought up a point that David had made when talking to me earlier—that the Heure Exquise ("urr eggs-KEEZ") was perfect for the cocktail hour: "So if your mother . . . *drinks*," I said, my voice betraying a tinge of desperation, "it'd be a nice choice."

"That's a good idea," she said.

In the end, though—some twenty minutes after she first arrived at the counter—she decided not to go with the Heure Exquise.

But she did buy. To wit, a 3⅓-ounce bottle of the *eau de toilette* Charlotte (one hundred dollars).

Ka-*ching!*

·······················

MY HOURS SPENT in the rarefied, musky world of fragrance had shown me that I could sell, or help to sell, an inanimate object; but could I sell something . . . more personal?

$\mathcal{A}$RE YOU A GREAT TELEPHONE ACTOR? a flyer, taped to the wall of the reception area of a company I will call Chatsworth, challenged me. Featured on the flyer were color photographs of a man and a woman; both individuals had the dewy, preorgasmic expression that we associate with those who inhabit coffee commercials.

But I had not come to Long Beach to work on a coffee commercial. Nor was I about to engage in anything as sophisticated as Cocteau's *La Voix Humaine* or any of those French film comedies of the thirties and forties in which white telephones are so prevalent that the genre is referred to as *la comédie de téléphone blanche*. No, no—mine was a far less sublime endeavor: I was responding to an ad that had run in a local paper reading, "Actresses/actors needed. Phone talent needed for party lines. Can you create characters? Do you have a great voice?"

Here was a golden opportunity to do some acting.

However, know this: I am not one to engage in graphic conversations about sex. Such conversations cause a reddening of my pallor; my face tends to look as if it had been tandooried. But mightn't the power of role play vault me over this particu-

lar barrier? Mightn't the protective armor of an assumed identity cause me to shed this inhibition? I wondered.

AMANDA, A MATRONLY, slightly huffy woman in her fifties
versed in the art of scarf magic, led me and two other male applicants—both well-dressed black men in their late twenties—
into her office. The office was tidy and barren of innuendo.
"No one's going to talk sex now, so you can relax," she told us; I
tried to heed her. "Now, about half the guys on the floor are
straight, and half gay," she continued. "You'll be passing yourselves off as members of the gay community. Does that bother
you?" This did not bother us. Explaining that "no one wants to
talk to a guy who's locked in a room answering a phone," she
said that the gist of the job was first to pretend that we had
called in as paying customers, and then to keep our interlocu-
tors on the line as long as possible. Indeed, bonuses to the
seven-dollar-an-hour salary would be paid on the basis of this
"holding time." Chatsworth's computers would automatically
disconnect callers on the party lines after twenty minutes and
callers on the one-on-one lines after ten; if they didn't, Amanda
explained, the callers would talk all night and never pay their
bill (the callers couldn't keep calling back: the computer would
screen out those who called too frequently). The discussion of
sexual acts involving animals, children, or sadism were ver-
boten. The callers were "looking for a top, which is a take-
charge guy."

Amanda's businesslike tone had been very calming. But as
soon as she used the word *top*—gay slang for the penetrator, as
opposed to the penetratee—I felt a little uncomfortable. Imagine your father's secretary telling you that a vibrator doesn't always satisfy her. You get the picture.

Amanda then asked me and one of the other applicants to

wait outside her office so she could talk to us individually. Was this our audition?

The first thing Amanda said to me when I sat down across her desk from her was, "So tell me about your outdoor activities—hiking, camping, biking." Outdoor activities had been one of Amanda's leitmotifs during our group interview; callers were apparently looking for someone "outdoorsy."

"I grew up in Massachusetts, and I camped out a lot," I said.

"I love Massachusetts."

"The Berkshires are there, and the Appalachian Trail runs through the western part of the state."

"Yes, yes," she said encouragingly.

"I like hiking. I ride a bike a lot. I'd take a twenty- or thirty-mile ride most days."

"That's considerable."

It struck me that my conversation was without the element of danger or suggestiveness that might yield high holding times. What did Amanda expect from me, though? I wasn't sure. Did this part of the interview still fall under the "no one's going to talk sex now, so relax" umbrella? How should I, metaphorically speaking, turn the heat up? For reasons not entirely clear to me, the phrase *valve poodle* popped into my head, but I had no idea what it meant, let alone how to graft it onto any of the wholesome imagery I had so far constructed. So I punted.

"I ride . . . fast," I said.

"Good. That East Coast thing is great," Amanda responded. "The guys love someone from their own time zone."

"Okay."

"Other sports?"

"I've played a lot of soccer."

"Soccer: good. Or they might get into something technical like gear or snowboarding—you just go with it. You love all that stuff."

Amanda offered me a full-time job on the swing shift—from 3:30 P.M. to midnight. I accepted.

"Are you sure you want to bother with this?" Amanda asked me after telling me not to worry, she would not be calling any of the references on my résumé.

"It sounds interesting," I said. "I have a lot of characters I want to try out."

"It's a great job while you're getting some other career going."

"I see it as an acting gig," I said. "I'm gigging."

"Yes, it's good experience."

"I have a contemporary monologue I can do if you want to see more."

"No, no. But I'll need you to do a day of training on Wednesday or Thursday."

I TRAINED ON Thursday along with two other men (one from my group interview) and six women, most in their twenties and thirties. Hunkered down in the fluorescent classroom, we took pointers from Barney, a bearded, ironical TCR (telecommunication representative) with several years' experience. Barney was a font of suggestions and guidance. Define your character as specifically as possible—measurements, occupation, romantic history, preferred positions. When asked how recently you have had sex, "Don't say, 'Two weeks ago.' That takes no time. Tell a story." If a caller alludes to his proclivities, investigate, and then turn your character into the kind of person he is specifically looking for. Do not employ the terms *describe* or *tell me* as either will identify you as a professional. Be prepared for a certain number of callers who refuse to speak; in these instances, launch immediately into a fantasy—something along the lines of "Guy I Met at the Beach," "Montreal Is Crawling with Bisexual Photo Assistants," "My Kitchen Counter Is a Very, Very Interesting Place."

The group then created an imaginary character—Barbara, a blond nurse from San Francisco, five feet eight inches and 125 pounds, 32-26-32, recently estranged from her boyfriend and looking for action. Barney then went around the room and asked each one of us one of the twenty questions most commonly asked of TCR's (e.g., "What are you wearing?" "When was the last time you were with someone?" "If you were with me now, what would you do to me?" and "Can I have your number?"). We were to answer as Barbara and try to draw our answers out. I was asked a fairly easy question: "What do you look like?"

"I'm five feet eight, a hundred twenty-five pounds, thirty-two, twenty-six, thirty-two," I rattled off. "A lot of people say I look like Meg Ryan, the actress from *Top Gun* and *Courage Under Fire,* only I think my sister actually looks more like her. What do you look like?"

"Okay, pretty good," Barney said. He then asked Rick, who was sitting next to me, "Do you swallow?" Panic flashed across Rick's heterosexual face.

"Unh, I'll take you for a ride, definitely," he said, tentatively. "You have to be ready for me, and . . . be ready to go on a ride."

"You didn't answer the question," Barney pointed out. "Barbara, do you swallow?"

Rick thought a minute. "Let's just say that I'm not an expert but I get the job done."

What?

Barney encouraged Rick to think about this question, and others like it, in the privacy of his own home. Would evasive answers yield high holding times?

During the break, I perused the orientation handbook. In a section called "Understanding Your Caller's Needs," I found a typology of callers, from "Your Average Fantasy Caller" to "The Cross Dresser" to "The Friendship Caller." The last type to be described was someone called "The Golden Shower Caller." The description ran, "This caller enjoys being urinated on or urinating on others. Good luck!"

I showed this to Brenda, one of the other trainees. "Does this mean that . . . ," I started, unsure how best to phrase my concern. "Is this guy going to, unh, pee into his telephone?"

"Whoa," she said, eyes widening with amazement. "He better not."

"Yes," I concurred, injecting a note of world-weariness into my voice lest Brenda think me a rube, "that's a big turnoff of mine."

"HAVE YOU DONE this kind of work before?" my supervisor, Andy, a Caravaggioesque urchin in his late twenties, asked me as we walked toward the room in which all the male TCR's sat.

"No, but I'm an actor," I said. "I trained at the Royal Academy of Dramatic Art in London."

"You did? Did you like London?"

"A lot. And I think the training will really help me out with this job."

Running along three of the room's walls were desk spaces partitioned off by four-foot-high carpeted walls; in the middle of the room sat a console where the supervisor would sit looking at a monitor that detailed each TCR's holding time. Seven TCR's, all on headsets, were working the lines when we walked in; among them, two were idle, one was conducting a lengthy monologue about news anchormen, one was drawing out his caller on the caller's former sexual partners, one was taunting, "I'm gonna get you, Daddy's gonna get you," one was feigning orgasm while squirming around in his chair, and one was feigning orgasm while playing solitaire at his desk.

Andy sat me next to Luis ("Daddy's gonna get you"), a bearded, heavyset fellow with a deep voice, and instructed me to listen in while Luis took half an hour of calls on the party line and then half an hour of one-on-one calls.

Chief among Luis's gambits was his ability to turn the clever and manipulative statement "This is costing us a lot of money. Let me get a pencil so I can write down your number and call you back" into a veritable *Oresteia* of holding time. He would put the caller on hold and then punctuate the holding time with breathy, urgent appearances—Luis supposedly picking up the phone in various non-pencil-bearing rooms throughout his house; Luis, having finally secured the pencil, breaking its tip; Luis, upon being given the phone number, lapsing into the throes of acute dyslexia.

I asked Luis if he was an actor, and he replied in the affirmative. "I could tell," I said. "You have a wonderful sense of commitment."

"Thanks."

After I had listened in for an hour, Andy told me, "Now we're going to break the umbilical cord."

I nervously plugged my headset into a party line and, with a TCR named Johnnie listening in, took a call. I thought it wise to keep my first character fairly close to myself, so I was Steve, a tall, blond, twenty-four-year-old photographer's assistant who was lounging around his New York City apartment in his underpants. My first caller was Rich from Ohio. When, twenty seconds into our conversation, I asked Rich what he was doing tonight, he answered in the manner that 90 percent of the fifty or so callers I would talk to during my sixteen-hour career as a TCR would: "I'm strokin' it."

Indeed, Rich was not a man with a surfeit of small talk; Rich wanted to penetrate Steve, and to do it with a certain amount of speed. (Callers were paying between four and six dollars a minute.) I accommodated Rich, saying, "Oh, yeah" some twenty times during the course of our four-minute-and-twenty-seven-second call. When Rich bleated softly at the conclusion of our imaginary lovemaking, I remembered something Barney had said in training: "Don't expect a thank-you. They just hang up." Rich just hung up.

That I had been operating under the assumed identity of Steve had been hugely liberating. Yes, during our call, I had hunched as far over onto my desk as possible lest my colleagues hear me; yes, my flushed cheeks at the call's conclusion were like a subtle reference to the treasures of the tandoor oven. But, given that I had just simulated sex with a total stranger while an additional total stranger listened in on headset, I was remarkably calm. Such is the power of role play. It had not been me who had been rendered a blithering, inarticulate mass of sex pudding by Rich; it had been Steve.

"That was pretty good," Johnnie assessed. "But you want to try to do more prechat with them."

"He wasn't really the chatting type," I remarked.

"It doesn't have to be general interest. It can be about sex."

"Okay," I said. "It might have helped to have established a location. We didn't really have a Where."

Johnnie disengaged his headset from mine, and off I sailed onto the seas of sex. I tried a variety of new identities. I was Eddie, a not-so-bright gym bunny in Los Angeles; I was a terse gentleman who referred to himself simply as "the Bear"; I was Derek, a British rocker who wanted either to "bung" you, to "bung it out of you," or to "bung you until you forget your name."

I loved being the Bear. "What do you look like?" one caller asked me after I had told him my name was the Bear.

"I'm six feet four, weigh two-sixty," I said.

"You're big."

"Thus the name."

A pause.

"Do you want the Bear to touch you?" I asked.

"Yes."

"Where do you want the Bear to touch you?"

"Everywhere."

"The Bear has been hibernating, but now he is aroused. He is putting his paw on your shoulder and pushing you down on the forest floor."

This call lasted eight minutes; at its conclusion the caller—clearly a caller who knew that he was talking to a paid operator—asked if, when he called the next time, he could request the Bear.

I knew that my Chatsworth superiors would frown on my ursine reverie—after all, you were supposed to evince the caller's fantasy, not force your own on him; moreover, the Bear could be construed as a form of bestiality, which we had been warned was illegal. But I couldn't allow these concerns to crimp my style. What surprised me, though, was that this caller was not only willing to have sex with a big, smelly animal, but that he was willing to pay off-Broadway prices to do it.

I WAS FURTHER pleased that the caller had responded to the Bear because the average Chatsworth caller tended to display a dispiriting lack of specificity.

"I want you to lie on my bed," Joe from Los Angeles said.

"Okay," I demurred. "What kind of sheets do you have?"

"I don't know. They're not silk."

"Cotton."

"Yeah."

"Like a pima cotton?"

"Sure."

"Do we have a thread count?"

Silence.

"It helps me get in the mood," I explained. "Knowing the details."

Click!

Joe had hung up.

Indeed, many callers saw fit to terminate my services well before these services's logical conclusion. This, according to supervisor Andy, was going to hurt something called my "efficiency rating." This worried him. "You're getting slammed," he told me. Are any of these people staying on longer than a minute?"

"Not many," I reported. "Some are hanging up after only fifteen seconds."

"Your efficiency rating is about 20 percent," he said. "The hang-ups are really hurting you."

Some of the hang-ups, my fellow TCR's explained to me, were regulars who knew they were calling a service and who were looking for their favorite voices.

But in most instances, the abruptly terminated calls seemed to be a response to my less-than-molten discourse. Take Sean from Georgia, for instance. Sean from Georgia had told me/Steve that he was a teacher. Did I want to make it with the teacher, he wondered. Sure, I said. Foreplay led to oral pleasuring, which led to Sean asking, "Do you like it with the teacher?"

"Oh, yes."

"You're going to get a good grade."

"I hope I get an A."

"Oh, you will, don't worry."

"I wrote my paper on *Mrs. Dalloway.*"

Click!

PRIOR TO THE commencement of work, the TCR's of each shift would meet in the training room to decide who would work "Party" (party lines) and who would work "Chat" (one-on-one lines).

"Welcome back, Hank," Andy said when I showed up in the training room for my second night of work.

"Thanks."

"You want Chat?"

"Sure."

"The only thing is, you were getting a lot of hang-ups on Chat, so I'm worried about your efficiency ratings."

"It's only my second shift," I pointed out. "This is like my out-of-town tryouts. I'm still workshopping."

Andy's face betrayed a small amount of confusion; he said I should start out on Chat and then switch to Party. I preferred Chat because there were fewer interruptions. Moreover, each Chat call was preceded by a prerecorded "tag," an insinuating, low-pitched male voice that clued the TCR into what specific line the caller had called in on. Most of the Chat calls I took were preceded by "Faaaantasy" or "Baaaarely Legal" (meaning the TCR was to claim he was nineteen years old), but I also had a "Boooodybuilder" and a nonsexual "Just Chaaaat." But you can imagine my surprise when the prerecorded voice trilled, "Maaaature Doctor." Stifling a burst of laughter, I quickly hit my mute button and asked Johnnie for clarification.

"Give him a physical," he said.

The randy older man of medicine was not a character I had prepared or one I had any experience with. But I couldn't leave the caller on hold; I had to jump to. My brain coughed and sputtered and, unable to generate a full picture, instead offered up a passel of random elements—a young man in a white hospital smock. Bourbon-flavored lollipops. Licking the stethoscope, in the manner of a suction cup, before applying it to the patient's person. Shaky hands, a wilting bow tie, moldering yellow teeth.

I pressed the mute button.

He was gone.

A dark day for medicine.

I attempted to beguile John from Tulsa by embellishing upon my physical characteristics. I told him, "I have very large hands. You should see me bone a fish: like a zipper."

"Yeah?"

"Yeah. Or skinning a badger? I'm The Upholsterer."

John from Tulsa was not fascinated by this information and proceeded to hang up, but not before dropping his phone on what was or was not a twenty-five-quart Calphalon stew pot.

Andy switched me to Party. Part of the difficulty of being interrupted on these lines was that I always felt it incumbent upon me to bring new callers up to speed—"Hey, Eric. I'm Ed, and I'm talking to Don from Boston, who thinks he's bisexual and who's just offered to put his hand down my pants."

The lovemaking, too, was difficult to negotiate. Grant from Long Beach—a sweet, gentle individual who had been vaguely interested in my opinions about the filmography of Joel and Ethan Coen—and I were slowly building to a crescendo when the bullying Mike from Dallas burst in on the line wanting to know if I had a roommate.

"Yes," I said, wanting to appease. But fearing that Mike might ask me to produce said roommate, I added, "But he has a girlfriend."

"Is the girlfriend hot?"

"They're both hot," I said.

I returned to the dialogue with Grant.

Mike interrupted. "Where's the girlfriend?"

"She's in France," I said. "Junior year abroad in France."

"Get the girlfriend," Mike said.

It occurred to me that producing the girlfriend for Mike would not only tax my powers of impersonation but would also signal to Grant that I was a professional. So I ignored Mike and concentrated on Grant. Fifteen seconds later Mike asked again, "Where's the girlfriend?"

I ignored him.

Another ten seconds later, "Where's the girlfriend?"

"She's not here, man," I said, irritated. "Grant is here, and he wants to get to know you."

"Put the girl on!"

I would be disingenuous if I did not tell you here that Mike intimidated me, even scared me. The Chatsworth offices were rife with security measures in the form of guards, cameras, ID badges, and ID codes, yet you couldn't help but feel like some aggrieved caller might somehow figure out where Chatsworth was located and try to gain access. So, my mounting fear dovetailing nicely with my thespian instinct to play, as it were, to the room, I took a deep breath and dove in.

"Zis ees Jeanne-Marie here," I said in a heavy French accent.

Oh, my God, I thought, momentarily panicking, I said she was *in* France, not *from* France. Idiot.

Click!

That was Grant. I knew it was Grant before even asking aloud for him. Grant had been patient and intelligent and had indulged my enthusiasm for *Fargo,* and now I had humiliated him. In his eyes I had abruptly metamorphosed from a moderately buff, culturally literate New York City photographer's assistant into a hideous swirling evil.

"I like French girls, Jeanne-Marie," Mike said.

Yes, and you probably like to melt the crotch off of Barbies, I wanted to say, but I repressed the impulse.

"It's just Marie," I vamped. "Most peepuhl are saying simply 'Marie.' "

"You sound kind of like a guy."

Now, what the hell kind of a statement was this? I didn't think Mike was deluded enough to believe that Marie really existed. Yet here I had sacrificed my call with Grant, had invested the time and effort in creating Marie, and now this jerk was going to throw stones at me?

"I . . . I have a very large jaw," I tried.

"Do you like big dicks?"

"I sink ezpecially ze American men are concerned about ze size when for me eet eez more about a man's sense of himself, yes?"

Mike was interested in performing cunnilingus on Marie.

"Oh, yes, I am an enjoyer there, Mike, but I am feeling right now like taking it somewhat slower."

"You don't like to rush things."

"No, I am, in this . . . I am escargot."

Mike sighed aloud. Then: "Okay, now do British transvestite."

"Wha—?" I started to ask, taken aback.

"British trannie!" he barked.

I slammed down the mute button. In retrospect, I'm not sure why I felt so scared at the time, but for whatever reason, my heart was pounding. My mind flashed to the application I had filled out and left with Amanda—what if Mike got my home phone number, I thought; what if he started lurking outside my house with a pair of large gardening shears?

By an hour later, however, my fear had given way to irritation—irritation with the callers' monomania and their inability to apprise me of their current or future activities without resorting to "I'm strokin' it." In fact, so inured was I to the charms of this statement that, when asked what I myself was doing, I started telling callers, "I'm preparing a small garden salad." (One caller hung up; two glossed over the statement; and one offered to "dress" my salad, a statement so repulsive to me that I pressed the mute button on him so as to allow him to be overcome by feelings of existential dread and then disappear.)

I knew I had reached the end. I was actively repelling callers. Lonely men were reaching out into the cosmos, and I was telling them that the cosmos did not contain them. I felt somewhat guilty. Some of these men, to be sure, were closeted and/or lived in small towns, and phone sex presented them their only opportunity to assert their homosexuality. Too, I felt like I was capitulating to my anxiety instead of just getting the job done; I could hear Patterson chastising me for my nouveau riche therapy bullshit. But deep down I knew that my work here was done.

The next day I called Chatsworth's offices from home and resigned. A supervisor named Jay took my call; I told Jay, "I think my work isn't hard-edged enough for your audience. I think I was boring them."

"You need to return your headset in five days," he told me.

"All right," I agreed. "I'm sorry it didn't work out."

"It happens," he said.

"I guess I was expecting something more Chekhovian, more metaphorical," I said.

"It's not for everyone."

"But, in my own defense, I have to say, a lot of your callers aren't creating a Where. They're just having sex in undefined space."

"Okay," he said unsurely.

"But thanks for giving me a shot."

"Sure."

AT LEAST TWO of my undertakings as a performer had had repercussions that I would not have anticipated at the outset. After I studied Shakespeare in London, I became engrossed by the mechanics of fight scenes and developed an appreciation for the Jackie Chan oeuvre. And after traipsing through New York in my pajamas, I started to think about my dotage, and to spend an unhealthy amount of time looking in mirrors while I tried to uncrepe my eyelids. But neither of these would have the potency or hold on my imagination that the repercussion stemming from my phone-sex experience would; even today, it is rare that I pick up a ringing telephone and don't think I'll hear a prerecorded voice growling, "Maaaature Doctor. . . ."

$\mathcal{W}$HILE MY STINTS as a purveyor of fragrance and phone sex kept my acting skills fluid, my movement skills had atrophied. My days on the Graham dance floor were far behind me. It was time to reacquaint myself with the Danskin crotch panel; it was time, once again, to make a dance.

I AM MADE uneasy by any activity that causes me to slough rhinestones from my person. I am rarely moved to lift any of my female friends up over my head and then proceed to pivot rapidly. I am not eager to have a group referred to as *scrutineers* watch me perform something called "the progressive twinkle." Yet when I learned that the International Olympic Committee had granted ballroom dancing provisional status as an Olympic sport, something was triggered in my brain. Call it false bravado, call it latent patriotism, all I know is that I suddenly longed to represent my fellow Americans while wearing the formal wear of our nation.

I hear you skeptics sniggering in the back row—the ones who would grant no seat on the Olympic Village tram to an aspiring Arthur Murray. Might I point out, however, that a recent study shows that the energy required to dance the quickstep for ninety seconds—the quickstep being only one of ten dances that Olympic ballroom dancers will probably have to dance—is about equal to running eight hundred meters? Also, consider that past Olympics have included such "sports" as stone-throwing, club-swinging, ice-carving, and tug-of-war.

I called several dance schools in New York City and explained that I was a novice interested in being groomed for the Olympics; I settled on a studio called DanceSport (DanceSport is the official name for ballroom and Latin dancing), where Al Pacino had learned to dance the tango for *Scent of a Woman*. The administrator asked if I had a partner (no) and how tall I was (five feet ten inches). She also explained that, in order to compete, I should have a working knowledge of five "smooth" dances (waltz, fox-trot, quickstep, tango, and Viennese waltz) and five Latin dances (cha-cha, rumba, samba, paso doble, and jive). I gulped. To execute a Latin dance with aplomb, you need to be housing a caged panther; sadly, my own animal spirit is more akin to an albacore.

DanceSport, on upper Broadway, is a three-story amalgam of mirrors and blaring music and dancers exhorting one another to "work it, girl." For $690 I bought ten private lessons, nine group lessons, and unlimited access to the school's nightly practice parties. During private lessons, I was to dance with my teacher; during group lessons, the teachers would pair the group off; and during practice parties, I would be required to endear myself to strangers.

I met my teacher, Reba, and was relieved that she was not a bitter Eastern European intent on using a metal-tipped cane to discipline my ankles. Rather, she is an ebullient, thirtysomething dancer who applauded my Olympic fervor and who was unfazed by the fact that it takes seven years for a sport granted provisional status to get on the Olympic program. "We better get started right away," she averred. While five other private lessons went on around us, we juddered across the dance floor in a fox-trot. When I nicked Reba's calf with my toe, I apologized, "I, unh . . . I bring a lot of raw energy to my work."

At the end of the lesson, Reba filled out an evaluation form. Next to "Confidence," she wrote, "Excellent," saying, "Because you're ambitious." Next to "Footwork," she wrote, "OK"; and next to "Continuity," "Will develop."

WE PROCEEDED, OVER the weeks, to negotiate our way through the basics of the ten competitive dances. Reba employed much visual analogy throughout—we were door hinges; we were the FTD florist; we had one-hundred-pound babies on our shoulders; we were tango stalkers intent on a big tango kill. Some conclusions I came to on my own: when you waltz, you should look wistful and vague in a nineteenth-century way, as if someone had told you to portray one of Chekhov's three sisters but then not told you which one. If it is a Viennese waltz, you should add a note of doom: you have arrived at the Vienna train station and remembered that you do not like sausage.

Meanwhile, in group lessons and at the private parties, I was reinforcing my new skills. I was also perusing the pool of attractive young beginners, hoping to find my Torvil or my Dean, hoping to induce in some stranger a desire to stand on a tall box with me while a public-address system blared our national anthem. But nothing clicked. Then one day, several months after my first lesson, something exciting happened: Reba said that she thought I was ready to compete. Pulling a sheet of paper out of her notebook, she showed me the dates and locations of three upcoming competitions. I was floored. I imagined receiving a sloppy, champagne-fueled kiss from a toupee-wearing sports commentator named Dick; I imagined filming a minidocumentary about how my Russian coach had plunged off her patio moments before the competition.

But who will I dance with, I asked. Reba said, "Me."

The gauntlet had been cast down. I signed up for another battery of classes; Reba choreographed routines for us in rumba, waltz, and tango. We learned the progressive twinkle (while waltzing, you point your feet in one direction and then slide them in the other). I was practicing wherever I could—on the roof of my building, on the beach, in my sleep. The song that we often waltzed to at the studio—"The Rainbow Connection," from *The Muppet Movie*—came to haunt me. One day Reba complimented my tango; I explained, "I've found my inner dancer. His name is Eduardo." Reba applauded this discovery and thenceforth told me whenever I should "use Eduardo."

In our last class before the competition, Reba, in an uncharacteristic show of nerves, simplified our routine significantly. "There are only two things I want to see at the competition," she told me. "Good posture. And don't get in my way." I experienced a slight sense of panic. Had I been abusive? Was I a toe-crusher and inveterate groper? I had no distinct memory of choreographic insensitivity. Over the course of the lesson, my shame metamorphosed into pique. When our conversation turned to our wardrobe for the costume, I asked Reba, "How dressed-up are you going to get? I mean, are you going to wear *face jewelry*?" She said she was not.

Moments later, in order to get an objective appraisal of our partnership, Reba asked Lori, the manager of the studio, to watch us rumba; Lori said I looked stiff and, reminding me that rumba is the dance of love, explained that my dancing should "tell the story of love." That night I returned to the studio for a practice party and tried to tell the story of love with various DanceSport students, including one in her late sixties whose parting shot was "Well, it gives you a chance to practice, anyway." Another student encouraged me to smile more, saying, "Judges *do* read face, you know."

Reba and I decided to perform our waltz routine at the pre-competition exhibition held at the studio the night before the main event. "There'll be other couples, yes?" I asked Reba; she assured me there would be. Riding the subway to the studio, I felt slightly jittery. When I walked into the ballroom, I saw that some 130 students and teachers had crowded into the room to watch the exhibition. My stomach was rendered a stormy tidal basin of dyspepsia. My bowels collapsed. Consider: it's fine to fail in front of friends, they will always love you; it's fine to fail in front of strangers, they may never know you. But to fail in front of people with whom you share a vague connection, to fail in front of someone with whom you have tried to tell the story of love—that is surely hell. We danced. There were other couples. I fled; lightning would be faster, except it zags. The evening remains inextricably linked in my mind with the phrase *weltering abdominal cramps*.

⸻

THE NEXT MORNING we drove to the New York Dance Festival competition, held at the Kismet Shriners Temple in New Hyde Park on Long Island. We arrived at about ten o'clock while the eerie "J couples"—junior couples, or children—were dancing; there are few more bracing sights than that of eight-year-olds, tarted up with mascara and sequinny formal wear, mamboing and hustling by the early light of day. Reba and I scurried down to the basement, slipped into our dance clothes, and started running through the routines. Although I took solace in the fact that we were competing in the lowest-ranking category, Newcomer, Reba said I seemed nervous. I tried to bluff: "That's just surface tension. Underneath, cool as a cuke."

We went upstairs and commingled with the hundreds of competitors from the twelve other participating studios, a group united by their shared passion for the immovable hairdo. The female competitors were swathed in Day-Glo, bell-shaped gowns that were equal parts Easter Bunny and wanton lampshade. Off the dance floor, whenever a non–gown-wearer approached a gown-wearer, he would look down at the dress's prodigious feather flounce and veer slightly away, as if in the presence of a potentially zealous pet.

"Be careful of that one," I said to a fellow dancer at one point, pushing him out of the way of a rapidly approaching gown-wearer. "Yeah," he replied. "Or she'll sequin us to death."

⋯⋯⋯⋯

CALL IT BEGINNER'S luck, but in our first heat we waltzed with true aplomb. Magic. A poem. Liquid gold. However, the judges gave us only second place out of four couples (ballroom uses placement judging rather than impression judging; competitors are ranked, not rated). It was an injustice. Surely we had done better. I wanted to protest, but what recourse did I have? A terrorist action, waged by my countrymen in ski masks, would have been overkill. I tried to let go of my ire lest it jaundice our other heats. But so dark was my cast of mind that, when we couples were lining up for our tango heat, I tried to voodoo the most accomplished-looking of my competitors by claiming that the dance floor was very wet. As soon as I uttered this, I was shocked at my brazenness. What had come over me? I had apparently let go of Eduardo and given birth to Tonya. But my gambit failed: the woman said that she had already been told the floor was slippery, and that many of the women were wetting down the bottoms of their shoes with Coke or water.

Our slightly sluggish tango took third out of three. Frustrated, I watched other heats for a while. When one competitor said of a tall, elegant dancer on the floor, "He has something," it was Tonya, not me, who remarked, "Yes, but unfortunately it's dandruff."

⋯⋯⋯⋯

HAVING EARLIER IN the day spent no small amount of time gazing covetously at the competition's two-foot-tall Connelly Charm trophy, awarded in recognition of "facial animation" and other "charm qualities," it was with great pleasure that I then spotted the trophy's namesake—one Ellen Connelly, the competition's organizer. I walked over to her, introduced myself, and explained that I was headed for the Olympics. I congratulated her on the turnout. I admired her dress. I gushed, "The trophy is *beautiful*."

Given that we were going to be uncontested in the rumba, I told Reba that, during that heat, I was working "strictly for the Connelly." (Reba's bombshell reply: "Start exuding.") We took to the floor and commenced dancing; my face was a very pageant of charm qualities and unrequited longing. There was animation; there was nuance. I cannot attest to my dancing, but I knew—even once it was clear that the judges were not going to reward me for it—that I had, facially speaking, achieved a personal best.

....

JESS AND I were in the kitchen, making dinner, which we would eat while watching *Key Largo.*

"So you don't want to be my partner?" I asked.

"I'm not sure I'd be any good," he said. "Are *you* any good?"

"It's strange—with all this performing I've been doing, I find I'm almost always as good as I'm expected to be."

"What do you mean?"

"Well, for instance, Reba gives me a huge amount of encouragement and support, so I am pretty good when I dance with her. But when I dance with anyone else—like some stranger at a dance party—"

"Things fall apart?"

"Yeah. Poultry in motion."

....

I SPENT THE two weeks after the comp—as I had learned to call competitions—in a funk. My dancing had gotten lazy. I was not hitting my marks. My spirit ebbed low. I had hit the wall; but deep down I knew that the only solution was to rumba right *through* the wall. And so, during the two months we had to prepare for our next comp—the Constitution State Challenge, to be held at the Sheraton in Stamford, Connecticut—I threw myself into my training with renewed vigor. When, at a wedding I attended, a friend asked me to dance with her, I tried to beg off. "This is *social* dancing," I said, fearful that overexposure to that crude art would dull my competitive edge. My reluctance to exhibit my burgeoning talent was compounded by the fact that the designer I had been hoping would design Reba's and my Olympic outfits—Vera Wang, who designed Nancy Kerrigan's sparkly Olympic duds—was at the wedding. My friend and I danced; I tried to obscure myself as much as possible.

I had doubled my weekly lessons with Reba to two hours; I mastered the difficult hip gyration known as Cuban motion; I added a red-sequin cummerbund to my waltz and tango outfit; I subscribed to *Dance Beat,* the monthly tabloid of ballroom. I was, more than ever, going for the gold. I would out-Fred even the nimblest Astaire.

AT THE SPANGLY, bugle-beaded maelstrom that was the Stamford Sheraton, Reba and I danced an admirable rumba in the pre-Bronze category and took first, beating one other couple. Then, while Reba went back to New York on Saturday, I spent a tense day waiting for our other two heats. On Sunday, fearful that I had lost my momentum, I overcompensated: I smeared Coke on my shoes for traction. This caused my shoes to pick up several tufts of yellow plumage off the stairway carpet; the sole of my right shoe looked like it had been in a car crash with Big Bird. Neither of Reba's and my other two heats were exceptional; as *Dance Beat* would put it, my floor craft was uneven, and I was chesty through my topline.

In between heats, I chatted up other competitors, eager to find other Olympic contenders. When a slightly haughty competitor—a man whose epicene glamour brought to mind the union of a Scandinavian pop star and a large, angry lizard—suggested that I, now thirty-three, might be too old for the team, I told him that I was already talking to Bulova about endorsing me. "They're thinking about strapping a wristwatch to my heel," I said.

The man responded, "You must be really good." I explained that, although it is possible that I will never be considered one of the all-time great ballroom dancers, I am an engaging ballroom *stylist*.

I WAS REMINDED at this precise moment of something that Carrie Fisher once told *The Star Wars Insider* about making *Star Wars*. "The last line of the script," she said, "was that the princess is way down the hall and she is 'staggeringly beautiful.' I crossed off the 'ly' and 'beautiful' and felt this new wording more approached what I could bring to the character."

As I looked out over the dance floor, the word *staggering* still reverberating in my head, I had a premonition that this episode of my life was drawing to a close. But this sense of impending finality was not without a measure of satisfaction—I felt, overall, that I had met the challenge ballroom had posed to me and had in so doing, been broadened. I had found Eduardo and, on the basis of this discovery, was led to believe that I might be able to find other men lurking within me, too—perhaps a swaggering, overcaffeinated FM-radio disc jockey eager to dispense "hot licks" and "ear candy"; or an alcoholic former clown with some novel entertainment ideas for children's birthday parties; or Earl, a corrections officer from Staten Island.

But would anyone ever pay me to find them?

CHAPTER 14

*H*UNKERED DOWN IN a booth, my friend Kevin and I were running lines at Doaba, a diner on First Avenue just north of Chicago City Limits, where I had befriended Kevin in an improv class. The lines that we were running were from a sketch I had written in which I had taken phrases from actual phrase books for travelers and strung them together into a narrative; this undertaking had occurred to me when, glancing at *Teach Yourself Catalan* in a bookstore one day, I had been surprised to discover that, among the Catalan phrases that the writers of that book felt we future travelers to northeast Spain and the Balearic Islands required, was the rather dire

   I am prepared to raffle the goat.

Kevin and I were at a point in the sketch wherein our characters—a traveler in an unnamed foreign country and the friend he has met up with there—were addressing a waiter in a restaurant, using phrases I had found in *Teach Yourself Urdu in Two Months*. Rapid-fire, but speaking softly so as not to disturb the other three patrons in Doaba, we were alternating phrases,

This meat is underdone.

This potato is overcooked.

This cup is broken.

This bread is stale.

This meat is bad.

This orange is very sour.

Then we both chimed in together for

The pears are rotten and we have had to burn them.

Just as we said this last sentence, the waiter—the living, breathing one from Doaba, not the one in the sketch—walked over to us and, slightly scowling, asked, "Can I get you anything else?"

"Unh, no thanks," I said, unsure if the irritation that we seemed to cause him was specific or general. I asked for the check and then, for good measure, said, "Everything was wonderful." He nodded matter-of-factly. I left a three-dollar tip on a six-dollar check.

Given the hour—about 9:30 P.M.—and the fact that Kevin lives half an hour away in Queens and I live half an hour away in the Village, I suggested that we continue rehearsing out on the sidewalk.

The best light outside was emanating from the restaurant's far window, where, seemingly, we would be out of the sight of the waiter and the diners. Kevin and I took our places and started running through the sketch. Passersby glanced at us sideways but did not break their stride.

Kevin was doing an admirable job, finding nuances that I had not imagined in the writing of the piece, but I thought there was more juice to be extracted from our *German Chit Chat* exchange. In it, I asked

What is the matter with Louisa's neck?

and Kevin replied

It seems to be something cancerous. The girl is very delicate, there is always something the matter with her.

It was the "very delicate" part that I thought required exploration. We tried various amplifications—hostility, wonderment, bafflement—before settling on despair. Yes. Perfect. Just then, ready to run through the whole thing one more time, we happened to glance behind us and notice the waiter standing in the window.

"He was staring at us," Kevin reported.

"I hope we didn't offend him," I said.

"I don't think so."

"He's so grim, though," I noted. "'What is the matter with the waiter's neck?'"

I WILL GRANT you that to rehearse in a restaurant a sketch that takes place in a restaurant is decidedly "meta." However, let the record show that the sketch was to be *performed* in a restaurant, too. Not just any restaurant: Elaine's. Literary mecca Elaine's, long the eatery of choice for tweed-wearers like Jay McInerney, Tom Wolfe, and David Halberstam; Elaine's, where cast members of *Saturday Night Live* bump up against *Esquire* editors in their efforts to ogle Woody Allen.

How had this turn of events come to pass? I was watching television at home one day when came a ripple on the pond's placid surface. My telephone rang: the organizers of the Toyota Comedy Festival wondered if I, in conjunction with my friend Mark O'Donnell, wanted—for pay!—to be part of the festival's "Literary Laughter" reading series. To be held at Elaine's.

Now, I don't know about you, but I often have a certain hesitation about literary readings. If ever there was something to remind you of your friend Darva, the one who edits a poetry journal called *Gauzy Touchstone,* the one who corners you in the kitchen during a dinner party and confides in a hushed whisper, "The October issue of *Gauzy* is dedicated to the victims of the North Ridge earthquake," this is it. The air is thick with the perfume of noble intent; the audience, 90 percent of which is other writers who will at some future date give readings, too, is chiefly in attendance in an attempt to incite reciprocity.

But surely a reading given at a comedy festival—a comedy festival underwritten by an adorable car—would neatly sidestep the grim. Moreover, the other participants in the reading series were an illustrious crew—George Plimpton was going to do one night; Roy Blount, Jr., another. Flattery threatened to curl my eyelashes. I couldn't agree to the engagement fast enough; Mark was interested, too. And why conform to the strictures of the literary reading, I thought? Why not write a sketch in which a traveler is so beset by mishap that he is forced to raffle a goat? Why not put together a Spalding Gray–type monologue about my adventures in the world of competitive ballroom dancing, to be memorized and to employ the term *chesty through my topline* as often as possible? After all my theatrically fringey activities—selling perfume, being a phone-sex operator, et al.—here was a chance to do some real performing.

THE FIRST POINT of order was a name for the event. Jude, the woman organizing the event for the festival, thought we should be billed as "Two Guys from *Spy.*" This seemed a stretch—my stint as a *Spy* staff writer had taken place eight years ago; Mark, a former contributing editor, is far better known for his plays (four original ones produced off-Broadway and two adaptations of classic French farces that Bill Irwin directed at the Roundabout), novel (*Getting Over Homer*), and collections of humor.

"Is there some other billing we can think of?" I asked Mark over the phone one day. "I've been taking all these acting classes; maybe there's a theater theme."

"We could do 'Obscure in Many Fields.' "

"That's fun. Or what was that one you used once—'Mark O'Donnell, Guy of Letters.' "

"Sure, we could be 'Guys of Letters.' Or what about 'Leggy Super-Authors'?"

" 'Leggy Super-Authors.' I like that."

"We're both kind of tall."

"Yes."

I called Jude with this new name, which she seemed to like but not love. Moreover, she wondered if there wasn't a third writer, a more notable writer, "maybe someone like Paul Rudnick," who could join us. She explained, "I've talked to the powers that be, and they like the Elaine's events to be sort of sexy."

And not like two inebriated Boy Scouts mumbling "doo doo" and "I can wiggle my penick" into the microphone.

"Rudnick would be amazing," I said of the playwright-turned-screenwriter (*Addams Family Values, Jeffrey,* and *In and Out*) and former *Spy* contributor. "But I bet he's hard to get."

If you are gay and witty and literary and call New York your home, you live in perpetual contradistinction to Paul Rudnick and NPR commentator David Sedaris. From high atop the parade float that is witty bitchery these two preside, their outstretched hands oscillating gently in a royal wave, their tiaras delicately coated with baby oil to induce extra sparkling; down below we darty-eyed pretenders mill about, springing to life only to nip at heels or to generate bilious rumors.

Jude and I thought of other writers, both *Spy*-affiliated and not, who might be willing to join us: Sedaris. *New Yorker* columnist Kurt Andersen. Freelance snarler Joe Queenan. Author/*Spinal Tap* cast member Tony Hendra. Roz Chast collaborator Patricia Marx. *The Official Preppy Handbook* author Lisa Birnbach. *All in the Timing* playwright David Ives. I offered to fax her a list of names; she said, "Please. I'm on a deadline, so if you have phone numbers . . ."

Would we lose the gig if we were unable to produce an entity larger than ourselves? Although Jude was enthusiasm itself, I couldn't help but feel like I was standing behind the cordoned rope, trying to drop a name that would magically grant admission. My hunch was that she would put out calls to Rudnick, Sedaris, and Andersen, then cancel the booking if none of these three jumped. But each of these three merited his own sparkly Toyota evening; to perform with Mark and me would most likely be either a favor or a lark. Did I want to volunteer their phone numbers in the fax, thus enabling Jude to tell them that she had gotten their numbers from me, and putting the onus of the favor on me? Did I choose this particular battle? I supposed I could call Mark and ask his opinion, but to do so seemed to make more of the matter than necessary. So, through a highly complicated form of mathematics, factoring in my limited history of favors and compliments I shared with these three, then factoring in the limited history of favors and compliments that I imagined *Mark* had shared with these three, I provided only

Rudnick's phone number in the fax but wrote next to it, "Please don't tell him that I gave you his number."

A week later I had not heard from Jude, so I figured we had been axed. Dead.

Five days later I received the glossy brochure for the Toyota festival in the mail. Racing through it, I saw that Janeane Garofalo was performing at Irving Plaza, and that Al Franken and Arianna Huffington were performing in midtown. Then, nervously glancing at the column describing the Elaine's events, I saw Mark's and my names, followed by the subheading "Two Guys from *Spy*."

Relief. We were on.

....

"VERY AUSPICIOUS," JESS said when I told him about the Elaine's booking.

"It should be fun. I only worry about noise," I said.

"How so?"

" 'Veal piccata on table six; veal piccata, table six.' "

Jess wondered aloud whether Woody and Soon-Yi would be in the restaurant that evening.

"Necking quietly," I imagined.

"Mm-hmm."

"I hope they sit in the back if they do," I said. "Incest can be *very* distracting in the smaller venue."

We had already run into Mia; and now Woody and Soon-Yi. Could a weekend with Tony Roberts be far in the offing?

....

ONCE I HAD written up a version of my experiences as a competitive ballroom dancer, I memorized it and started to rehearse it at home. This went fairly smoothly. Mark being the far more illustrious and accomplished of the two of us, I had offered to open for him; thus I needed patter or a curtain raiser to start the evening off with. I devoted my energies to a song that would poke fun at the fact that, per Toyota's decision, admission to each of the Elaine's readings would be ten dollars. Granted, these monies were to go to New York City Literacy Volunteers, but nevertheless, to charge admission for this type of entertainment, some of which is to be read off of pieces of paper, is pushy. My days as a ballroom dancer had left the plaintive, plunky-plunk banjo stylings of "The Rainbow Connection" echoing in my head, so I wrote new lyrics, whose chorus ended, "So if you feel itchy/Disappointed or bitchy/Talk to the man in Japan."

I loved rehearsing the phrase-books sketch with Kevin. Playing the much put-upon traveler, I was afforded the opportunity to voyage from mild irritation to irritation to hostility to vengefulness to glee. Quoting from *Russian Without Toil*, I got to upbraid Kevin

Accursed cabman, I am sure that we are late!

and then, moments later, I became haughty and exasperated as I cited the *Baedeker Traveler's Manual of Conversation:*

That is very dear. Such a price frightens me.

One night, during our rehearsal at Kevin's apartment in Queens, it occurred to me that we would profit by trading roles once—that he should be the traveler, and I should play the friend, the accursed cabman, and others. This helped. Kevin brought a wonderful sense of bafflement to the moment when the traveler, upon seeing a bolt of lightning strike the man sitting next to the driver of a horse-drawn carriage, yells from a Russian phrase book

Our postillion has been struck by lightning!

And it was I, all modesty aside, who found the note of eerie urgency required of Kevin's role as the car-crash bystander from the *Fanagalo Dictionary*:

One European is dead; another has a broken arm, and a baby is bleeding from the mouth and ears.

So authoritative and funny was Kevin as the respondee in one of the *German Chit Chat* dialogues—

—Why do you not play with Willibald?
—Because I don't like him.

—that I thought about rewriting the sketch so that I could have this line. But something told me that this way lay madness; start rewriting the material in your favor, and before you know it, you're upping your year of birth and airbrushing your head shot.

While riding the subway home from Kevin's, I started to worry that, while the sketch was novel, it was highly contrived and thus held the risk of making us look like we were sweaty laborers in the comedy vineyards. The next morning I ran through the song and the ballroom monologue. I was visualizing the evening as follows: Song. Ballroom monologue. Phrase books. Introduce Mark. Mark. Mark had kindly asked me to perform with him a sketch he'd written—we are to be two drunken, Michigan Militia types at a bar. I was enthused and flattered.

But after running through the song and the monologue four times each, my anxiety about the sketch started to seep into my feelings about the other two offerings and suddenly I decided:

kill the song. I can't kill the phrase books, I realize—the world must hear Kevin discourse about Louisa's neck; I must have the opportunity to scream, "Our postillion has been struck by lightning!" in front of a large group of people.

I worried about the song. The song might be construed as obnoxious, and it might alienate some of the audience, particularly its more politically correct constituents. Does the song dispute the notion of charitable contribution? Also, its slight xenophobia is compounded by the sketch's rather intense xenophobia.

Chop went the blade on my career as an aspiring Muppet.

————————

A HALF HOUR before we were to go on, I showed up at Elaine's, jittery but energized. Under the guise of using the men's room, I swept through the dining room on a Woody–Soon-Yi patrol: not in the house. Unlike my attempt to get the Queen in for a reverse command performance at RADA, this VIP no-show was a relief. Soon I was introducing Mark to Kevin and Kevin to Jess, being, as much as possible, a purveyor of gush. The room where we were to perform adjoined the dining room and was the size of a small studio apartment; at its far end, a Toyota Comedy Festival banner hung over a stool and microphone. Over the next twenty minutes, most of the thirty-two seats in the room filled up—eight with friends and colleagues of Mark's, seven with friends and colleagues of mine, and the rest with that group most desired and sought-after by performers: people you do not know.

Having apprised some of my Chicago City Limits classmates of the engagement, I hoped some of them would turn out; indeed, ten minutes before showtime, a turbaned Vivica—a fiftysomething woman in our class given to exciting headwear-based experimentation and bouts of sudden memory loss—

swooped into the restaurant; I greeted her, whereupon she gazed at me and said, "Unh, I'm having a sudden memory loss . . ."

"It's Henry."

"Henry, yes. Nice to see you."

The show lasted an hour and ten minutes. I got us off to a rocky start—the ballroom monologue elicited few laughs, and my resultant nervousness caused me to forget a large chunk of it. Some ninety seconds into the monologue, I looked out into the audience and their expression of tremulous, twinkly-eyed anticipation made me think of beleaguered travelers who are in close proximity to cups of hot, restorative coffee; four minutes later it was clear that I had spilled that coffee on their faces and persons.

But I plowed onward, onward. Then I called Kevin up to the mike, and we launched into our piece. In a word, boffo. From the early moment wherein my traveler spoke to Kevin's innkeeper from page 148 of *Spoken Yemeni Arabic,*

I did not sleep all night. The next time I want a drug.

to the moment, after heavy rains and flooding, that we shared from *Introductory Course in Spoken Hindi*

—*Perhaps you got flu.*
—*Oh! What a hell!*

we unbosomed tens of snorts, guffaws, chuckles, and titters. Flush with the rousing spirit of ambition achieved—yes, my emotional dial was decidedly set on Auto-Kvell—I introduced Mark and proceeded to lap up his wonderfully sly comedic wares, jumping up midway to perform his sketch with him.

"I loved that phrase-books one," one woman in her early forties said to me as the audience filtered out onto the street at evening's conclusion and one of the event's organizers handed me a check for one hundred dollars. "I spent a weekend in Paris that was exactly like that. Almost word for word."

"That goat raffle must have been tough," I said.

"Harrowing."

CHAPTER 15

*G*OOD NEWS COULD not have come at a more opportune moment. Having just flown to Rhode Island's Block Island in a wee airplane, I was feeling slightly rattled. As usually happens when you fly on a plane that is smaller than your apartment, the pilot had asked me, prior to departure, how much I weigh, thus forcing me to quiet the voices within me that were screaming, "This should not be an issue!" The only passenger, I had sat next to the pilot and, once at flying altitude for this fifteen-minute flight, had watched the pilot flip on the cruise-control switch, reach for a stack of papers and manila file folders, and then proceed to engage in an activity that I instantly recognized as "light filing."

I am not a nervous flyer, yet given the proper materials, I can find that in me. So, upon deplaning, it was with a slightly shaky hand that I called my answering machine back in New York and found a message from Adam Dolgins thereon.

Adam is an attractive, thirtysomething fellow whom I worked with at *Spy,* where he was the marketing director. He subsequently wrote a book, *Rock Names,* about the origins of various rock bands' names, and had gone to VH1, where he is a writer and producer. Personality-wise, the keynote to Adam

Dolgins—*The Adam Dolgins Experience,* if you will—is dry commentary wedded to intense calm. Now, I do not mean here, in stressing the attributes of dryness and calm, to liken Adam to an underarm deodorant. No, no—it would require a far braver man than I to say, "Every time I think of the man who gave me my break in television, I am reminded of the Mennen Speed Stick." Rather, I mean to evoke a certain stead-fastly-steering-the-ship-through-the-fog quality; you have the sense with Adam that, were a gigantic fissure suddenly to rend the earth below you, swallowing buildings and the unsuspect-ing, that Adam—and, by implication, you—would watch it all crater-side, exuding dry calm.

Adam was looking for on-air correspondents for the pilot of *Viva Le Rock!* (later to be called *Rock Candy*), an irreverent newsmagazine show he was making for VH1. And so, four days later, I found myself at the Viacom building in Times Square. If you watch MTV, you know the Viacom building and the way it appears to be perpetually surrounded by hordes of teenage fans emitting squeals audible only to dogs. On the twenty-first floor I found the door to Adam's office in the middle of a glass wall; the design metaphor of the VH1 offices is Early Squash Court.

Whisking ourselves downstairs, we hunkered down in a booth in the Lodge, the Adirondack-style cafeteria where em-ployees of Viacom—including VH1, MTV, and Nickelodeon—break bread. Adam showed me a list of approved segment ideas that he had pitched to the VH1 brass. As I scanned down the list, the one that most appealed to me was showing five or six of the same rock videos to two groups of people outside the rock-and-roll demographic—kids at an after-school program and then older folks at a senior citizens' center—and then contrast-ing their opinions, to comic effect. In discussing the idea with Adam, I discovered that he, too, is a fan of *Duplex Planet,* the "If you are an old man and you go into a bar wearing pajamas, people will buy you drinks" zine that had partly inspired my pajama-wearing.

The more we talked about the idea, the more I wanted to do it. Yet given the urgency with which acting or performing-based opportunities had sped down the street toward me with arms wide open, only, upon contact, to plunge through a sewer grate, I worried. It would behoove me, I realized while sitting here in the Viacom commissary, to self-promote. But how? Adam was familiar with my magazine work, and had seen me on *The Tonight Show,* so he didn't need to be beaten about the head on either of these fronts. But interviewing groups of people about their taste in music—why me?

It occurred to me that people have always liked to confess things to me. I told Adam this.

"Really?" he said, his interest piqued.

"Yeah," I admitted. "I have sort of a monsignor quality."

He called two days later to say that we would be proceeding.

————

THESE WERE EXCITING times in which to work for VH1, as the network had just started to come into its own. Started in 1985 with the purpose of staving off competition for MTV, VH1 (short for "Video Hits One") had lacked a defining personality in its infancy, relying on a strange brew of old sitcoms, Julio Iglesias videos, and stand-up comics accompanied by either puppets or melon. But when John Sykes took over as president of the channel in 1994, he ushered in a programming formula—pure music and music-related shows for adults—that had turned the network around. Now, in 1998, not only was the breakout hit *Pop-Up Video* discussed by the cognoscenti and its style imitated by advertisers, but VH1 boasted cable television's highest concentration (86 percent) of eighteen to forty-nine-year-olds, advertisers' most desirable viewers. It had also extended its subscriber base to more than 62 million homes, thus putting it within arm's reach of first-tier cable channels like CNN, ESPN, and MTV and their 70 to 73 million homes. Among its fans and supporters was none other than President Clinton, who had been particularly taken by a series of specials the network had aired on Elvis Presley, and who had donated an old saxophone to Save the Music, the network's campaign to raise money for school music programs.

On a personal level, I welcomed the challenge inherent to television hostdom—avoiding the false enthusiasm that we associate with purveyors of televisual cheese. I would try not to ripen into human Brie.

EACH OF THE two shoots took about four hours. The kids that I interviewed at the 92nd Street Y ranged in age from eight to twelve; the folks at the Clinton Senior Center ranged from sixty-three to ninety-four. In each instance, we assembled chairs in front of a TV monitor on which we showed seven videos; I stood beside the monitor and asked questions, some written by Adam, some that I ad-libbed, about the videos' content, style, and relative merits. The videos we showed were Michael Jackson's "Black or White," Madonna's "Take a Bow," the Spice Girls' "Say You'll Be There," the Rolling Stones' "Love Is Strong," Hanson's "MMMBop," and Mariah Carey's "Honey."

While I cannot say that I took to my tasks as moderator/host like a duck to water—one of my friends, upon watching the segment, felt compelled to tell me, "There's a difference, you know, between deadpan and just plain dead"—it took me only five minutes or so at the first shoot to realize that I liked the job immensely. What intrigued me was having to constantly negotiate and define the relationship between the group and me. Was I their confessor? Their accuser? Their friend?

Their coach? All was uncertain. This uncertainty beguiled. I also liked the fact that I was allowed to generate some of the material. Casting a backward glance over my somewhat threadbare career, I realized that I had the most fun when I was afforded the opportunity to conduct, and sometimes derail, the train.

Some things however, were not uncertain. For instance, it quickly became clear that, like a good straight man, I could set up jokes for the group members. I asked the seniors, "If Michael Jackson were your son"—a big, easy puffball from the pitcher's mound—whereupon one of the more outspoken women in the group barked, "I'd spank the living daylights out of him!" Ker-*pow*, a homer. But there were also times when it was best to interfere as little as possible. When the dapper seventy-seven-year-old gentleman told me that he found the Madonna video "romantic," he quickly found himself in a verbal tussle—a highly telegenic verbal tussle—with the woman sitting next to him, a fiercely opinionated Asian woman of regal bearing.

"You call that romance?" she said sourly. "I don't call that romance."

"You mind if I talk to the man?" he asked her. "I'm not arguing with you."

"This is a discussion group, my dear! Are you the authority?"

"To *him*," he coached her. "To him, not to me."

"I'm talking to him," she reported.

"Well, you talk to him."

"Why, of course!" she barked.

"All right."

People were talking.

Three

ESS HAD BEEN offered a job in Los Angeles. The offer had come from Endeavor, an agency representing writers, directors, and actors, started in 1995 when four agents at International Creative Management opted to hang up their own shingle; Endeavor was now looking for someone to open a book department, the chief duty of which would be to sell the film rights of books to producers and studios. This is what Jess had been doing for Curtis Brown, a tweedy, older agency in New York that represents exclusively authors, but going to Endeavor was an opportunity to enter the Hollywood maw. And to enter that maw from solid ground—although young, Endeavor had already proven a fierce rival to agency stalwarts Creative Artists, William Morris, and ICM; Hollywood insiders were referring to it, in *Variety*-ese, as the industry's current "hot shop."

I encouraged Jess to take the job. My magazine work is wholly transportable, and a move across the country would in no way impede the ready exchange of lovingly wrought prose for delightful Condé Nast dollars; moreover, geyserlike, opportunities for performing blast out of cracks in the Los Angeles terra firma like sulphurous, slightly mustardy facials. But a move to Los Angeles, I knew, would be particularly good for Jess. Now, at last, he could don the proverbial coke spoon. Here was opportunity—opportunity regularly to stand in a Beverly Hills living room with a passel of television stars who are negotiating the set of tensions that lie at the intersection of ritual circumcision and heavy catering, opportunity to prove to the world that *package* is a verb.

Jess was going to the show.

On the personal front, the mood was more cautious. Although Jess and I had been together for seven years, and although we had spent almost every night of those seven years together, we had never actually lived together. The plan, with respect to our move westward, was for Jess to give up his New York apartment and to move all his furnishings over to mine, which I planned to keep, then for us to get an apartment in Los Angeles together. Would too-close quarters cause us to squabble; would we, exposed to each other's foibles on a constant basis, crave release or cessation? That it was our seventh year was particularly nervous-making; dangling over our heads like the sword of Damocles was the notion of the seven-year itch. Would we wander or stray, become isolated from our flock of two?

I AM NOT one of these New Yorkers who thinks that Los Angeles is a cultural backwater full of philistines, all of whose pants' waistbands are elasticized. In fact (stage whisper), I *like* Los Angeles. You need only drive the length of Mulholland Drive at sunset, or spend an afternoon basking in the cliff-lined seclusion of El Matador beach with a good book, followed by dinner at the funky Reel Inn, to know that this is a city that bears examination. Moreover, having grown up in a suburb, I find Los Angeles—which is nothing if not a series of suburbs—to be oddly reassuring. Many are the solaces of being able to stand barefoot on your lawn; many are the solaces of being able to fill the hatchback up with groceries.

But, for this sixteen-year New Yorker, the chief source of fascination regarding Los Angeles living is, of course, that now a washer and dryer would be located inside my domicile. Shortly after we had moved into our spacious, Spanish-style duplex near the Farmers Market, I found myself standing in front of these appliances and staring, dumbstruck, like prehistoric man hunched before his fire, or modern man his TV. The convenience that these devices afforded started to dazzle me, to haunt me, to distract me from all money-generating pursuits.

One day I did a load that consisted of a towel and a pair of socks.

I BECAME THE pliable helpmeet. Jess was working harder than he ever had and would come home exhausted and hoarse. I proffered back rubs and homemade meals, I generated backchat and banter. Jess's new position and our recent arrival in Los Angeles made us fairly popular, and more than a few times in our first few weeks we would have dinner with or go on some outing with a business prospect of Jess's—a glamorous development person in from New York, a producer with a deal at TriStar, a studio executive whose primary relationship with the word *creative* is to use it as a descriptor of the word *deal.* These outings could be fun, particularly when these people could be persuaded to unearth Hollywood anecdotes. Among my favorites that we heard was that of a young screenwriter who had pitched a movie idea to a very old, dinosaurish studio head.

"I like that," the studio head had responded. "It would be good for Sigurry Ray."

The young screenwriter quickly inventoried his own brain, and coming up with no match for Sigurry Ray, said, "I don't know who that is."

"You know," the studio head said defensively, "the girl from *Aliens.*"

"Oh, Sigourney Weaver!"

The studio head glowered at him: "Don't fuck with me."

WAS I BECOMING a Hollywood Wife? I will never be like Iris Cantor, who, faced with her husband Bernie's 750 Rodin sculptures, has said she felt a need to "soften up the art collection with paintings"; I will never be an avatar of rhinoplasty like Candy Spelling, or have my own fragrance like Tova Borgnine. I can, with a certain amount of ease, imagine the daily activities of someone like Sugar Rautbord—I see her dropping off her Smith & Hawken gardening clogs at a Rodeo Drive boutique so that an employee can hand-stencil them HERE COMES THE SUGAR! My life shares no similarities with theirs.

And yet I couldn't help but feel like the tenor of Jess's and my life together, or the individuals who peopled that life, was somehow changing. We were spending what seemed an eccentric amount of time hiking in canyons with entertainment lawyers.

CHAPTER 17

*I*NHERENT BETWEEN ANY two people who work in show business is an implied contract: if the other person is willing to believe—even though there is little evidence to support such a claim—that I am the next David Letterman, then I am willing to believe that he—although there is little evidence to support such a claim—is the next Martin Scorsese. But as soon as either party breaks the contract—as soon as he starts thinking of me as someone who can get him publicity because of my magazine contacts, or as soon as I absentmindedly introduce him to another friend as "Steve, a reader at Disney," then all bets are off. We love in direct proportion to how much we are loved.

The same applies to projects as well—at the outset, when I am being considered for a job, I think the project shimmers with potential brilliance; but as soon as I am rejected, the project is a redo of a stink bomb turned out in the early seventies.

So when I read in *Drama-Logue* that Radio City Music Hall Productions was looking for a "warm, jovial" singer, twenty-eight to thirty-two years old, of average size, to play Santa in its Christmas spectacular, I was flooded with both a revivified appreciation for the dazzling pyrotechnics of the Rockette kick-line and with thankfulness at this rare instance in which non-traditional casting would work in this white male's favor. I joined seven other warm, jovial, average-sized men in the crowded lobby of a rehearsal studio in North Hollywood; I felt twittery and excited.

"I'll take your picture from you," the bearded, fortysomething director told me once I had been called into the audition studio. He asked me my age; I said thirty-six.

"That's good," he responded, and used a Magic Marker to circle the *5'10"* on my résumé.

"How will the Rockettes figure in the show?" I asked.

The director and the casting director looked at me uncomprehendingly.

"Are the Rockettes in the show?" I asked.

"Yes," the casting director said.

"Will they be elves, or will they be reindeer?" I pried.

"They'll be the Rockettes," the casting director said, adjusting her earring.

"We'll have real elves," the director offered.

"Oh, good," I said, striving for joviality. "I have very strong elf skills."

"Such as . . ."

"Well, in general, I interact well with the differently sized."

The casting director did not respond to this statement, lost as she now was to the throes of earring maintenance; but the director smiled warmly, and I thought, You've got him eatin' outta your hand, kid. I launched into my sixteen bars of "I Wish I Were in Love Again" with brio—I envisioned Santa as having just run into a lissome Aleut fur trapper named Naomi whom he'd always had a thing for—but its conclusion met with a mere "Thank you." I was not offered sheet music from the show, as the auditioners who received callbacks had been.

As I shambled back into the lobby to get my jacket, I could

feel the enthusiasm drain from my body. A young, thin Santa? What an idiotic idea. That's as bad as those avant-garde directors who portentously announce, "We're going to do *Pajama Game*. Set in an African township. *Without the songs.*"

"Well?" one of the actors I'd talked to earlier asked me.

I reported, "No."

"Oh, I'm sorry," he said genuinely.

"Yeah, well, I hope they sell reindeer burgers in the lobby," I wheezed. The actor's eyes widened. I continued, "I hope Mrs. Claus scalds all the Rockettes' faces with hot cocoa."

"Hey," the actor said, trying to calm me.

"You know, the more I think about this whole thing, the more I think it spits *right* in the face of older character actors."

"Yeah?"

"Yeah. I hope Wilfred Brimley is very, very angry right now."

CHAPTER 18

"So we showed the show to a focus group," Adam told me over the phone one Tuesday afternoon. "Your segment tested really well. Through the roof. They said they'd never had such high scores for a segment before."

"Hubba hubba! Congratulations, man."

"Congratulations to *you*."

"It could have been anybody."

"The people in the group mentioned you, and said you didn't patronize or condescend."

"But the laughs don't really come from me."

"But you set them up."

"Yes, I'm a comedy *enabler*."

"The segment was *so* popular that VH1 is thinking of spinning it off into its own show. A special."

"You're kidding. So, like, show videos to a group of firemen, and then a group of arsonists?"

"Yes. Or a group of Boy Scouts—"

"And then the Michigan Militia."

"Something like that."

"And what about *Viva Le Rock*?"

"It's a go."

"Ba-da-*bing!* Congratulations."

"Yeah. Champagne, champagne."

ADAM SENT ME a tape of the *Viva* pilot and then called several days later.

"It looks like they want to go ahead with this *Rock of Ages* special, which would also serve as a pilot."

Our little comedy project had metastasized!

"There would probably be another host—a woman—and four segments," he explained, "one of which would be an expanded version of the one we already did. There's a lot of stuff we didn't use."

"Like the Asian woman saying, " 'Don't feed him' when we showed them Prince."

"Right."

"This is all so amazing."

"You could be the *Pop-Up Video* of 'ninety-eight, the breakout of 'ninety-eight."

"Sweet."

We talked more specifically about the pilot.

"I just watched the segment again," I said. "There's kind of a dead-fish quality to my performance."

"People in the focus group mentioned liking you. I think viewers are used to seeing stand-ups who come on and are really schticky."

"Yes, I'm antischtick."

"And what you read as low-energy, other people read as—"

"Irony."

"Right."

"I'll take it."

Editing can flatter. Lev Kuleshov, a Russian film pioneer born in 1899, realized this in the teens with his now-famous

"Kuleshov effect." Kuleshov shot some footage of actor Ivan Mozhukhin staring straight ahead without emotion, and then intercut this footage with stock footage of a bowl of soup, a barking dog, and a baby. When Kuleshov showed the edited sequence to viewers, they were highly impressed by how hungry (the soup), frightened (the dog), and caring (the baby) Mozhukhin looked.

I FLEW BACK to New York. It had been decided that, for my second segment on the pilot, I would interview three generations of an Italian-American family. A VH1 segment coordinator found the Russos, a lively family of eight in the Bronx. The Russos were encouraged to videotape themselves hanging around the house and then to send the tape to VH1. "There's a lot of bickering," Adam said of the tape. "Sort of a *Saturday Night Fever* feel." He mentioned a noogie fest.

The day before the shoot, Lauren Pollack, an associate producer, called from Adam's office. When she asked about clothing, I proposed two outfits; she said to wear one and bring the other.

"Also, I have a note for you," she said. "Calm and energized. Remind Henry to be calm and energized."

"Okay."

"Make sure you eat before we go. The house will smell like pasta, but we won't be eating there."

"Got it."

"Great."

"A friend is going to put a little eyeliner on me."

"What?"

"Before the shoot. Just a little eyeliner."

This was a lie. *I* was going to put a little eyeliner on me. I was going to put a little eyeliner on me in an attempt to connote zest. But, while I didn't mind alluding to my vanity, I was not anxious to allude to my *lonely* vanity.

"Let me tell Adam," Lauren responded.

I could hear them murmuring in the background; vague, low-intensity embarrassment started swirling in my head region. There was a second male voice in the background, too; I envisioned a burly network executive huffing, "Jesus Christ, is this kid gonna show up in a caftan?"

Finally, murmuring still audible, Lauren reemerged: "We love it."

"Oh, good. I showed the tape to friends, and they said, 'Eyeliner.'"

This, too, a lie.

"Adam says he assumed you always *have* worn eyeliner."

"Sort of a Perma-Lash situation?"

"Yeah."

"Actually, no."

WE SHOT AT the Russos' house for four and a half hours. Setting up a VCR and monitor in the living room, we positioned the eight family members—two grandparents, two daughters, and four grandchildren, ranging in age from seventy-two to eleven—on or in front of the couch.

"Do we have to act natural?" Danny, the chunky, spiky-haired eleven-year-old in an Ozzy Osbourne T-shirt asked me.

"Yes."

"So if my brother says he likes Hanson, I can hit him?"

"Just make sure you do it on camera, darling."

I tried, throughout the taping, to achieve smirklessness. I started out by ad-libbing, "This is a very special occasion, getting the whole Russo clan together. We hope that by the end of the taping you're all still talking to each other." Then, referring to the questions I had written the night before while watching the eight selected videos at my apartment, as well as the questions Adam and supervising producer Frank Gregory had written, I proceeded to fire away as the Russos tucked into a generous banquet of videos: "Criminal" by Fiona Apple, "Like a Prayer" by Madonna, "I Get Lonely" by Janet Jackson, "It's All Coming Back to Me Now" by Céline Dion, "Steppin' Out" by Tony Bennett, "Sex and Candy" by Marcy Playground, "Superfreak" by Rick James, and "Long Hard Road Out of Hell" by Marilyn Manson.

To give you just a tiny taste of the penetrating sociological insight that showing videos to groups of disparate ages can afford, I will now divert your attention to the hyperbolic splendor of the Céline Dion video, "It's All Coming Back to Me Now." In it, Dion is a chatelaine who, padding around her premises with a hairbrush one storm-tossed evening, engaging in copious amounts of hair care and hair management, is suddenly reminded of her erstwhile beau, dead from a motorcycle crash. We see the crash—lightning fells a large tree into which the motorcyclist plows, giving way to a fireball so large as to bring to mind the life work of Robert Oppenheimer. Upon being shown the video, the fortysomething daughter in the group started to cry, saying, "It's very emotional. I think she's great, better than Barbra Streisand." Her twenty-three-year-old son enthused, "Anyone in a strong relationship will really kick it with the video, totally"; when he said "kick it," he made, as intensifier, a downward motion with his fist that bespoke involvement with hip-hop culture. Young Danny, however, fixated solely on the pyrotechnics of the crash, labeling them "cool."

Bringing, as we were, videos of questionable taste, not to say merit, into the Russo home, I couldn't help but feel like an ambassador of low culture.

"If I was sitting in here, and my wife walked in and I had

this on," the grandfather said of Apple's "Criminal," a video in which the young singer is scantily clad and shown sprawled in a bathtub and on a basement floor, "she'd throw me and the television out the door."

"Is this art or is this . . . ," I started to ask, realizing as I did so that I was, to some extent, leading the witness.

"No, that's not art," the grandfather responded.

"What is it?"

"Pornography, actually."

I didn't happen to agree with him—to my mind, pornography is identified by its insistence on bad jazz guitar, people in police uniforms, and the premise that interactions between realtors and prospective tenants necessarily yield frantic copulation. And yet. And yet, were someone to fill my home with the sights and sounds of something that *I* considered pornographic —say, Martha Stewart double-coating terra-cotta planters with yogurt in order to incite premature mossing—I am not sure that I would be as gracious and friendly as the Russos were to us. They helped the crew move furniture; they laid out snacks for us on the dining room table; they encouraged us to use their phone; they were altogether patient and willing and generous.

THREE DAYS LATER, at the American Museum of the Moving Image, we were to shoot the "host wraps"—introductions to the individual segments on the show. During the ensuing three days, I tried on various occasions to say *host wraps* without reflexively thinking of cocktail wieners straitjacketed in dough. I was unable.

Upon arriving at the museum, I met my cohost, Emmy Laybourne, a tall redhead in her late twenties. Prior to our introduction, I knew little about her other than that she is a writer/performer who has done a lot of improv, and that her mother is Geraldine Laybourne, the former president of Nickelodeon who built that network into a powerhouse of children's programming and who then became president of Disney/ABC Cable Networks. As I stood and talked to Emmy in the hallway, I realized that I was operating chiefly out of narcissism: that this cohost was trying to find out who the other cohost is in an attempt to buoy his own cohostly self-esteem. It worked. Entirely of its own volition, my brain rattled off an Emmy checklist: Cute. Warm. Funny in an unexpected way. Leggy. Important mother. It dawned on me that I wasn't really having a conversation, I was looking into a mirror. The slight eerieness of all this was, seconds later, ratcheted up when she revealed that she lives with Sean Conroy, who was one of my improv teachers at Chicago City Limits, and that she has worked with Matt Besser, my improv teacher from Upright Citizens Brigade.

Self-love began to effervesce within my body like a delightful, possibly French beverage.

RETURNING TO LOS ANGELES four days later, I soon found myself watching more television than I had at any other time in my life. One week I watched three award shows, an event that engendered in me the fervent hope that God is not spending as much time helping people win awards as award winners would have us believe he is.

CHAPTER 19

*G*OD APPARENTLY HAD plans for me, too.

The minute I learned that I was going to be a the-ater critic on one of the hippest radio stations in the country, I worried that I lacked the requisite intellectual panache. To be a theater critic, I have always thought, you must ooze, or at least have the capacity to ooze, discernment and worldliness. It would not hurt, either, were you prone to withering pro-nouncements; you should be the kind of person who comes out with things like, "I've heard her 'I'm Still Here,' and believe me: she's not." When someone asks you, "Have you seen the new Neil Simon play?" you should be able to look your inter-locutor in the eye, take a beat, and then, deadpan, announce, "Probably." You should be able to approach a group of opera snobs, feel comfortable in their presence, and then, when you have determined that the group is discussing an opera com-pany whose artistic director once cut in front of you at the espresso counter at Bayreuth, announce, "The only purpose of that company's Ring Cycle was to remind us that fat people, when dying, cannot stop singing." A bow tie would not be out of the question; a bow tie, or even a cape. And when it comes time to name your column or radio spot, there should be only one viable option: "Meaner Than an Antique-Shop Cockapoo."

·····

WHAT HAD TRIGGERED this most recent reverie? A friend had been alerted by his colleagues at KCRW that the station was looking for a theater critic; people submitting names of potential critics were encouraged to "think outside the box"— the individual need not be a theater reviewer at present but might simply be amusing and "a fine writer-presenter."

If there is an epicenter of intelligent hip in Los Angeles, it is KCRW. It airs more NPR news than any station in Southern California and is considered the flagship station for the network. If, say, Vanessa Redgrave comes to Los Angeles and deigns to talk to a news source about her new project or career, she may very well grant that privilege to KCRW. So might Martin Scorsese. In addition to showcasing the jewels of the NPR tiara, KCRW offers a wealth of original programming, too— Harry Shearer, the voice of *The Simpsons*' Mr. Burns and a member of Spiñal Tap, is the writer and host of *Le Show;* brilliant musicians hold forth and sometimes play as-yet-unreleased tunes on *Morning Becomes Eclectic;* my friend Sandra Tsing Loh offers a hilarious weekly commentary called, of course, *The Loh Life.* Several times since arriving in L.A., I had been late for appointments because, while parking my car, I had fallen under the spell of some KCRW program on a topic I had heretofore not been all that curious about, like local politics or World Beat music.

In short, an oasis.

·····

ONE TUESDAY AFTERNOON I interviewed by telephone with two women from the station: Sarah Spitz, KCRW's publicity director; and Jacqueline Des Lauriers, a producer and the head of the station's community affairs and promotions. I explained to both parties that I have reviewed books for *Newsday,* the *New York Observer,* and *The Village Voice,* and that, after being a staff writer for *Spy* in the late eighties, I wrote a lot of humor for *The New York Times Magazine* and *Vanity Fair.* These facts did not repel them. I learned that three reviewers were going to be "auditioned," giving weekly reviews on a rotating basis for an indefinite number of weeks; the reviews would be four minutes long, would pay one hundred dollars each, and would be aired at a prestigious drive-time hour: 6:55 P.M. on a Tuesday, airing again on Wednesday at 3:00 P.M.

At the conclusion of my interview with Jacqueline, she said, "Well, there's always a first time. I'm game."

Hosanna! I was in! Soon I could dismiss Jason Robards as "just another Jason Robards impersonator"; soon I could cavil that the name Streep always makes me think of a French person asking me to undress.

This was every failed actor's revenge fantasy.

"And are you Los Angeles–based?" Jacqueline asked.

"I am. I just moved out in February. But I kept my apartment in New York."

"You never can be sure, can you? Don't buy a case of Coke; buy them one at a time."

The moment I hung up the phone, I looked down at my right hand: nerves had rendered it blurry. I might *think* I could be witty and arch with the best of them, but when you got right down to it, I was highly intimidated by the task. There were hundreds of important productions of plays and musicals that I had never seen; my ignorance of their merits and weaknesses suddenly throbbed in my brain. My thoughts: Am I qualified for this job? Will I be able to walk the fine line between trying to be fair and wanting to be funny? Is it a liability that I think most musical theater is a conspiracy to discredit gay men? Do I need to have strong opinions about Senecan tragedy? Will I need to know whether the use of knickers is historically accurate in the Jacobean revenge play? Such questions nagged. Moreover, I was all too aware of the theater critics who had been passed over; seizing an issue of *LA Weekly* and seeing the names of some of its reviewers, I thought, "All of these people will soon hate you." Was I being opportunistic? I couldn't help but feel like I was displaying, in the parlance of public radio, a startling sense of entitlement.

Eager to calm myself, I went for a walk through my neighborhood. Gradually, sanity prevailed—there was no reason to neurose over my lack of theater-reviewing experience, I realized; I was hired more as a humorist, so the only instance in which I should self-flagellate is if I'm not my sparkling zestiest or if I don't work hard enough. These feelings of rationality and optimism were buoyed moments later when, turning up La Cienega and entering Bookstar, I picked up an issue of *Travel & Leisure* and saw that a writer friend of mine had conned that publication into sending her and her husband to Portugal in search of white absinthe.

My friends were traveling through Europe in search of hallucinatory aperitifs, all on someone else's nickel; I was self-flagellating because I'd never seen Betty Buckley do *Gypsy* at the Paper Mill Playhouse.

Of course I'm qualified for the KCRW job, I thought. I'm a homosexual! I'm from New York! I own several bow ties!

....

HERE WAS THE next hurdle: it had been decided that my first review, or piece of commentary, was to be about a lecture at the Getty Museum that August Wilson and his colleagues were giving concerning their attempts to revive black theater in America. In the spectrum of possible topics for humor, this one scores low, down near Bosnia. But therein, I knew, lay the challenge: if you can make August Wilson funny, you can make anything funny.

You remember Wilson's back story: in 1996, he, the most accomplished black playwright in our nation's history, denounced color-blind casting, claiming that to cast blacks in "white" plays—say, to have a black Lady Macbeth—was to collaborate with the culture of racism. Differentiating between black art conceived to entertain white society and black art conceived to feed the spirit of black folk, Wilson called for the creation of an authentic black theater. He was taken to task by American Repertory Theater artistic director and *New Republic* drama critic Robert Brustein, who waved the banner of universal values and dismissed Wilson's views as "rabid identity politics." Others pointed out the hypocrisy of Wilson—a man who has only one black parent and who came into prominence through two not-so-black institutions, Yale and Broadway—being the movement's spokesman. On the eve of a New York City debate between Wilson and Brustein in February 1997, *The New Yorker* published an essay by Henry Louis Gates, Jr., in which Gates pointed out that there already is an authentic black theater—namely, those touring gospel musicals and broad comedies that are referred to as the "Chitlin Circuit."

I had seen *Fences* and *Joe Turner's Come and Gone* on Broadway, so my plan of attack, before going to the lecture itself, was to read a few more of Wilson's plays, then to download ten or so newspaper and magazine articles about Wilson off the Internet. Worried that nothing I encountered in Wilson's oeuvre would be a springboard for hilarity, I also looked at George C. Wolfe's parody of black theater, "The Last Mama-on-the-Couch Play," from *The Colored Museum;* I thought I might quote the moment when, the protagonist's melodramatic sister, Medea Jones, having wailed, "I beseech thee, forgo thine anger and leave wrath to the gods!" the son asks what has "gotten into" her. She answers, "Juilliard, good brother."

————————

GOING TO THE GETTY was a wonderful treat; it had just opened, and aspiring visitors had been making parking reservations months in advance. As I took the museum's tram up the hill to the spectacular white city above, I felt like I was entering the closing scenes of a science fiction movie; I envisioned bald men and women in flowing robes serving me lozenge-shaped food rendered from the city's cremated felons.

Wilson and his colleagues proved to be engaging speakers. While their presentations lacked the gossipy abandon that had heretofore made the Wilson-Brustein feud such a yeasty pleasure to behold, there was much to write about. To my relief, Wilson and his colleagues' mandate was not separatist; they mentioned twice the financial necessity of attracting the white audience. (I planned here to mention the dirty little secret of the 1960s Black Arts movement, wherein playwrights like LeRoi Jones and Ed Bullins had come to fruition: the movement was funded largely by the Ford Foundation.)

I had six days, more than ample time, to prepare my spot. Four minutes of airtime comes out to about six hundred words, about two and a half double-spaced pages. At first I found myself speaking my words aloud as I wrote them—the narcissist's version of moving your lips while you read—but then I realized that this was a dangerous, not to say precious, tendency—the next thing I knew I'd be writing exclusively with a fountain pen and referring to all my writing as "scrivenings." So I nipped this habit in the proverbial bud.

As I beavered away on my copy, two things rapidly became clear. Complicated sentences—not unlike the one you are currently inveigled in, dear reader—with intricate clausal configurations or too many ideas or commas: bad. Short sentences: good. It also struck me that two of my greatest weaknesses as an actor, low energy and a slight lockjaw, were, for a theater critic on public radio, advantages: the former would bestow upon me the slight air of boredom that we associate with many members of the NPR talent stable; the latter would suggest that I am a member of the Culturally Obliged. By Culturally Obliged, I mean those people who attend cultural events out of a sense of obligation rather than passion or curiosity. I mean those people who are always telling you, "I can't tonight. I have theater," their very language betraying the onset of disease.

A whiff of Culturally Obliged is not a bad aroma to emit, I thought: the Culturally Obliged see *everything*, particularly if it is seven hours long and both physically and intellectually arduous. I refer you to *Les Atrides* and to *Life and Times of Joseph Stalin*. Once seated for each of the four installments of *Les Atrides*, Ariane Mnouchkine's 1992 play about the House of Atreus, the audience was not allowed to leave the theater. *The New York Times* reported that when audience members at Robert Wilson's twelve-hour Stalin production at the Brooklyn Academy of Music found themselves recounting plot episodes that others did not recall—the production featured 144 untrained actors, many of them deaf and sixteen of them dressed in ostrich costumes—they were led to believe that the show's staggering length had caused them to go into a trance and then start to hallucinate.

<hr />

TWO NIGHTS BEFORE I was to tape my spot, I listened to one of the other auditioning critics—Lawrence Christian, reviewing *Chicago* at the Mark Taper. His delivery was effortless and his commentary well reasoned. Thinking craftily, I wondered how I might make myself different. Find the hole, fill the hole.

What wasn't Christian providing that I might be able to? Two commodities came to mind: comedic zest and cocktail-party fodder. By this second item I mean a factual nugget that listeners could repeat to their friends and colleagues in an attempt to feign depth. One of Wilson's colleagues—Victor Lee Walker II, a professor at Dartmouth—had had an interesting one: a 1965 *Ebony* survey had determined that the three African-Americans most influential to other African-Americans were Malcolm X, Martin Luther King, and Muhammad Ali. But when the survey was taken thirty years later, the three most influential were Michael Jackson, Mike Tyson, and Michael Jordan—or, as Walker described them, "an alleged pedophile, a convicted rapist, and an apolitical basketball player." I included this in my text. For comedic zest, I decided to make hay not with Wilson or his mandate but, rather, with the context of the evening. I poked fun at the typical theater lecturer (a logy individual "whose somewhat eerie presence seems to be attributable to equal parts dry sherry and lobotomy") and addressed the strangeness, after hearing Wilson and his colleagues' appeal for grass-roots activism, of tucking into Getty-donated crudités and Chardonnay ("you could almost hear a department-store employee intoning, 'Ladies, the fragrance in the air is Liberal Guilt' ").

The morning I was to record the review, I sat at my desk at home and read it into a tape recorder four times. My first impulse was to make it sound as relaxed and natural as possible, even if to do so was to inadvertently add pauses and several *uhhs;* the effect was "you have stumbled onto me in the bathtub, and I have a great deal to say about the future of black theater." Not ideal. Moreover, this version clocked in at four minutes, twenty seconds—twenty seconds too long. So I tried to add a sense of urgency. Yes. Better. Three minutes, fifty-eight seconds.

KCRW IS UNDERNEATH the cafeteria of Santa Monica College, in the basement. Many warrenlike offices stem off from a central corridor; the ambience says, "noble but underpaid." Having, that morning, donned my bicycle-chain-oil–besmirched khakis in an effort to convey "Thinks global, acts local," I walked down this corridor, found the recording booth, and introduced myself to J.C., the Jodie Foster–ish sound engineer. I wasn't sure of the procedure, and my mind was working overtime. Was someone going to read my copy before I taped it? Would my larynx implode upon usage? Would Linda Wertheimer emerge from the shadows, rip my copy in half, and scream, "Get off the bus, poser white boy!"?

No. I sat down in front of the microphone. I accepted J.C.'s offer of a glass of water. I donned headphones. I told J.C., "Let me know if I get spitty." We taped the review. We taped it again for safety. I thanked J.C. I left.

IT'S DIFFICULT TO describe how strangely and liberatingly intimate it feels to be on the radio. You're sitting alone in a dimly lit room. Headphones cut out all outside noise. There is neither spectator nor technician, neither audience nor cameraman in front of you. You feel as if there is nothing you wouldn't talk about or confess to. That many of your listeners are snugly enclosed in a moving vehicle somehow factors into it, too; I could envision my words emanating from a speaker on the car's door, wafting onto the driver's person at thigh level and then lodging themselves equidistant to flesh and panty hose. If doing comedy improv is like screaming at someone while you stand in his backyard, and being on television is like sitting down and talking to this same person in his living room, then being on the radio is like sneaking up on him while he's lying in bed and then whispering in his ear.

Ten minutes later I was outside, basking in the sunshiny embrace of a lovely late-spring afternoon. It occurred to me that I had been living in Los Angeles for four months and had not once been to the beach. I drove over to the beach at Venice, where I took off my shoes and walked along the water's edge for two hours. Sometimes life is good, I thought. Sometimes life is very, very good.

I CALLED MOM on Mother's Day.

"I'm auditioning as a theater critic for the NPR affiliate out here," I told her.

"Pursue that," she said. "Secretly that's what I always thought you would be. A theater or film critic. Do you have the job already?"

"They're trying three of us out, and then they'll pick one."

"Siskel and Ebert and Alford."

"Yes. I'm a less hairy Gene Shalit."

"Yes, you would be wonderful at that. Pursue that, and then dangle it in front of the *L.A. Times.*"

"Okay, boss."

It struck me that this conversation with Mom might be the perfect opportunity to come out of the closet, as it were, as a theater critic by trying out a few withering pronouncements. But nothing came to mind.

"Oh! I just found out we get PH1!" Mom enthused.

"I thought you did. It's not premium cable. It's probably right next to MTV on your dial."

"It's very *closely related* to MTV."

"Unh, yes. So the show is on June third at eight o'clock. I have no idea what it will be like. You might find it amusing, you might find it incomprehensible—"

"I'm your mother."

"So the bar is low."

"Well . . ."

"The bar is very, very low."

JACQUELINE CALLED FROM KCRW and wondered if, for my second review, I wanted to see a play in Pasadena called *The Old Settler*. I knew that this was a black play, and the part of my brain that is responsible for generating uncharitable comments flashed, "What next—*An Evening of Lorraine Hansberry*?" Anxious not to be typecast, I wiggled out of *The Old Settler* and was given instead two new American plays being done at the Matrix—*The Water Children*, written by Wendy McLeod, who wrote the Parker Posey movie *The House of Yes;* and a psychological thriller called *Yield of the Long Bond*, by Larry Atlas.

The chief "review" this reviewer had received when his August Wilson commentary aired had come from Jess, who had congratulated me and said, "You were wonderful. So erudite."

"Oh, thanks," I had mumbled.

"I thought you came off very polished, and very . . . erudite."

Jess had apparently found the review erudite. This was not a bad thing. However, when it came time to write and rehearse my second review, the little William Morris agent inside my head said, Go a different direction this time. Show that you have many, many colors; if possible, show that you have plaid.

And so I assayed, in my second review, to strike a more conversational tone. Moreover, rather than dwelling on the two new plays' thematic commonalities, a direction that might get turgid, I chose instead to focus on the fact that they were both double-cast. This is a Matrix tradition, which offsets the potential damage of actors leaving a show because of film or TV work, and which thus enables this small theater to draw auspicious talent (included in the casts of the two shows I was reviewing were David Dukes, Gregg Henry, Pam Dawber, Christopher Collet, and Wendy Makkena). The Matrix does not double-cast its shows so that Cast A appears one night and Cast B appears the next; rather, the actors are intermingled in various combinations. Inasmuch as a production of a play can be said to be a specific group of performances, then mathematics suggested to me that there were not *two* plays at the Matrix but seventy-three. I wrote about this phenomenon and then concluded my review by saying, "This is a theater that gives and gives and gives."

Down at KCRW, I sauntered to the booth, found J.C., and declined her offer of a glass of water: a bold assertion of my increasing self-reliance. The fortysomething Sarah, who had initially contacted me about the job, bustled through the booth, warm and lovely and full of praise for my first "spot"; moments later the witty sixtysomething Jacqueline came through, too, wearing a pale blue suit covered with clouds: if Magritte designed clothing. Jacqueline asked, "Do you know what you'd like to do for your next one?"

Los Angeles is full of hipsters; collect the goatee hair in any given neighborhood and you could carpet Nebraska. So when Jacqueline asked what I would like to review for my third spot, I suggested Justin Tanner's new play, *Coyote Woman*. Justin Tanner is a local playwright with a cultish following, many of whose works fall under the rubric "slacker comedies." I had already seen three of his plays since arriving in Los Angeles and was eager to see another.

Several days after I saw *Coyote Woman*, I met with my friend Rob, who was in from New York. We were having drinks at a bar in Venice, and the conversation had turned to the topic of a friend of his, a graduate student specializing in French theater, who had recently performed an evening of scenes *en français*. I asked if the friend had displayed any of the earmarks of talent; Rob said, "Yes. A lot of range. But his French was abominable."

As soon as I heard the word *abominable,* complete with its fusty, slightly antiquated overtones, I had a strange premonition that I was on the verge of my first withering pronouncement.

"I can't even begin to tell you how bad his French was," Rob said.

And then it hit me: "His French was so bad," I pronounced, "that everyone could understand it."

CHAPTER 20

*J*ESS GREW EVER more vibrant from the galvanizing force of high-powered Hollywood agenting. He was exhibiting a certain amount of what in the animal world is referred to as "display behavior." Whenever he went to the gym, he wore his Endeavor T-shirt, and sometimes his Endeavor sneakers; trips to the beach brought out the Endeavor suntan lotion (SPF #8) and the Endeavor beach towel. Indeed, the Endeavor beach towel was seeing a lot of service. One day, at a barbecue at some friends' house, Jess got ten minutes out of the Endeavor beach towel and its fascinating ability to turn itself into a tote.

His enthusiasms were seismic. He *loved* the manuscript he was reading, but he *loved loved loved* the one he'd read over the weekend. Unbidden passions rocketed forth: we should all go to Italy for the weekend! Flights to Rome are cheap now! Many of the trails through the Apennines are both dangerous and rugged!

I couldn't keep up with his fixations. One night, driving down Sunset on our way home, Jess, his fingers tapping on the steering wheel, turned to me and asked, "If you were on a desert island . . ."

"Uh-huh."

". . . and you could have only *one kind of onion* . . ."

CHAPTER 21

"WE'LL NEED YOU at three-thirty."

Sometimes seeds planted in the past bear no-longer-desirable fruit. But when I walked into my office one day and heard the highly flattering construction "We'll need you" emanating from my answering machine, I allowed the message's assertion of need to supersede my skepticism. For, while the project in question—Bobcat Goldthwait's cable oddity, *Bobcat's BigAss Show*—had seemed a desirable venue a month earlier when I had auditioned for it, now, exposed to the harsh light of day, it began to smell more than a little like day-old haddock.

But: "We'll need you."

Duty called.

I HAD BEEN apprised of the audition via *Drama-Logue*—something about people with a lot of improv experience and a "bigass personality" needed for a new show on FX. Having many years ago seen Bobcat perform at the Bottom Line, and having found his act to be both politically astute and very, very funny, I am a fan. As for the Bobcat filmography—or, more accurately, as for that portion of the Bobcat filmography devoted to the hilarious hijinx of young men and women readying themselves to be defenders of the law—I say simply that a man has to eat.

The audition, held in a large, cluttered room at the Hollywood Center Studios, where MTV's *Loveline* and HBO's *Mr. Show* are shot, had been thoroughgoing. First we had been asked to fill out a questionnaire. It asked you to list five true but unusual things about yourself, to be used for a segment on the show called "Dirty Little Secrets." I surprised myself by being able to come up with five things that were actually true: "I was once audited by a narcoleptic IRS employee who fell asleep during my audit. A security guard once kicked me out of Saint Peter's in Rome. I have never broken a bone in my body. I'm not wearing underwear. I know Tammy Wynette's real name (Wynette Pugh)." Then we were to list three things about ourselves that are not true. I wrote, "I have a glass eye. I am Dennis Quaid's cousin. My nickname is Mr. Wiggle."

The two men running the auditions then pulled out a TV monitor and showed us an episode of the show. A chaotic, bumptious affair it was. The gist of it was that Bobcat, assisted by two ditzy dancers named Wing and Ding, selects people from the audience and then compels them to commit small acts of humiliation (e.g., wear a diaper while drinking from a bottle, dress up like sumo wrestlers and wrestle) in exchange for prizes.

Here was a gig. Here was that most rare opportunity—to receive recompense for your improv skills. That the show was a burlesque—that, in order, to succeed on the show, I would need to sound the barbaric yawp—only made it, at the time, seem more desirable.

"You want to be over the top," we were encouraged. "The people who are the biggest hams are the ones who will win."

Then, one at a time, each of the nine auditioners was

brought to the front of the room and put through our paces. When it was my turn, the taller of the two men told me, "Be your favorite animal." I semisquatted, lifted my wavering right arm over my head, and started to whimper like a chimp.

"Now that animal having an orgasm."

My whimpering grew frenzied.

"You just won a million dollars!"

The chimp had, or I had? More likely me; I whooped volcanically and jumped up into the air.

"The IRS just took it away from you."

I contorted my face into a mask of agony; then I fell on the floor, sobbing.

"You're walking on hot coals!"

I bounced across the room.

"You're having a heart attack."

I grabbed my chest and, ever the vaudevillian, fell once more onto the floor.

"You're drunk and a cop pulls you over. Talk your way out of it."

I floated my head in a vague circle, finally locking eyes with the order-giver to say, "Officer, I was trying to get away from . . . the . . . big . . . truck." I contemplated plummeting to the floor yet a third time, but then I reconsidered: leave them wanting more.

I was then handed a photocopy of a Sydney Omarr astrology column and told to read the Pisces forecast first with a Valley Girl accent, then with a New York accent.

"Thanks so much. We'll let you know."

⸻

I REMEMBER WALKING back to my car and thinking I had fared pretty well, that my frenzied chimp had shown the signs of promise that my drunken motorist had made good on.

Moreover, something about the people connected to the show—a media hipness, I guess, or maybe the show's penchant for goofy satire—made me think that one of them might be familiar with my work as a writer. Indeed, as I climbed into my car, I imagined the casting people handing the executive producer a list of us actors who they had selected for the taping, and the executive producer, upon seeing my name, exclaiming, "Hey—this guy writes for magazines! I love his stuff!" I then also imagined—it is with not a little embarrassment that I relate all this to you—the executive producer picking up his phone and calling me. I heard him enthusing over something I had written and then asking, "Are you sure you want to do this, man?"

"You mean, be on the show?"

"Yeah."

"Of course. I'm a big fan of Bobcat's."

"No, it's just that, you could, you know, be *writing and producing* the show."

"I'm trying to do more performing."

"Okay, well, great. We're honored."

"No, no, thanks for letting me do it."

This imagined conversation would soon strike me as almost grotesquely naïve.

———

WOULD THAT MY memory banks were unencumbered by the subsequent *Bobcat* taping. Deprived of the details, left to your own devices to imagine the proceedings, you might paint your picture in broad and generalized strokes, and thus divest the incident of its specific grimness and horror.

But memory, on this occasion, is not so kind. All is firmly etched: the eighteen other contestants and I were, in groups of three and four, seated at tables at stage's edge. I sat with a college student named Rick, who would not talk to me, and a dancer named Charity Luv, who would talk only to me. I was chosen, along with a man named Ross, for the second scene in the third show to be taped that day. Bobcat pointed at the two of us and, to a din of applause and whuh-*hoo!*s, we ran up on-stage. Ross and I were then led backstage by a stagehand.

"Okay, guys, we're gonna put on a puppet show, like for little kids," said a short, brunette woman bearing two sock puppets, each with a blond wig and a bow tie. "Do any voice except a little kid's voice. Unbutton your pants." We unzipped our flies while the woman bearing the puppets explained the bit: by each putting our puppet-encased hand down our pants, we were to create the illusion that our members were engaged in a conversation. This conversation was scripted and written on cue cards; each of its ten or so lines featured a pun on the theme of erections or urination.

I BECAME INSTANTLY hostile and unpleasant. I thought about escaping the studio but knew that this would incur expense and trauma for the production. I like to think that my taste in humor is fairly catholic and can embrace both high and low. I like to think that, with the possible exception of fart jokes—I don't know, maybe it's just me, but I have never met a joke about human-produced methane that I felt truly *delivered*—I am, with respect to possible topics for humor, open-minded and expansive. But put in the position of having to speak penis puns, I realized: I'm not. I have my limits.

Wing, or Ding, said to me, "This will be funny."

"Yeah, it's very witty," I huffed. "Kind of like a Noël Coward thing."

She looked at me slightly irritably.

You could have ironed clothing on my cheeks, so fiery were

they with embarrassment; a soundman started to mike Ross and me, and I found I was unable to engage in eye contact with him.

My first impulse, with respect to the material at hand, was to deliver the lines in a heavy Cockney accent. But in the swirl of activity backstage—the soundman readjusting Ross's and my microphones, Wing and Ding negotiating the vagaries of their form-fitting costumes—I changed my mind and opted instead to play it like a stupid person who thinks he is being especially clever.

Moments later the cameras started rolling, and Bobcat introduced us as Dick and Peter. Ross and I sashayed to center stage and did our bit. Bobcat asked the audience, by show of applause, to select the "better" of the two of us. They chose Ross.

Five minutes later, for the "Dirty Little Secrets" segment, I was handed a blue notecard on which were supposedly written three of my secrets. But my secrets had been edited. They now read, "I once farted really loud in a job interview. I was audited by a narcoleptic IRS employee. I went on a blind date with a girl who was really blind."

Cameras rolling, Bobcat asked five of us to read our cards aloud and explain to the audience which one of the three statements was false. When Bobcat and the camera got to me, I read my cards but substituted *burped* for *farted*.

Moments later a sixth contestant, who had been sequestered backstage during our reading, came out. Bobcat, moving down the line of us notecard-readers, read each of our cards aloud so the sixth contestant could guess which of the three facts was not true. When I moved up to bat, as it were, Bobcat looked at my card and furrowed his brow. He read my first secret as "I once burped really loud in a job interview."

The sixth contestant took two guesses to detect my lie.

Backstage, handed a form from a company called Promotional Consideration, Inc., that informed me that I was to win an Ashley Comfort Leather Lounger and Ottoman valued at $199, I scrawled across the form, "I wish to forfeit this prize."

As I WALKED toward the studio's exit, I saw Bobcat shambling down a linoleum-tiled hallway. He's so much better than this show, I thought. I looked into his soulful eyes; they bespoke a hundred network executives saying no, a hundred casting directors scribbling "Not quite right," a hundred talent show bookers thinking, Maybe. Maybe as a backup.

I snapped back to consciousness, suddenly wondering if, yet again, I was talking mostly about myself.

Bobcat shot me a sly grin. I extended my right hand and shook hands with him.

"Hey, I'm sorry I changed that *fart* to *burp*," I said. "But I won't be complicit in a fart joke."

"No—hey," he said, all forgiveness and charm. "I changed it, too."

CHAPTER 22

NASMUCH AS MY burgeoning career in the performing arts was an opportunity to express myself in a visual medium, my burgeoning career in the performing arts was also an opportunity to hover anxiously over my nonringing telephone. Having not heard from Adam in almost a month, I called him. *Rock of Ages* had been picked up for six episodes. Adam apologized for not having sent me a copy of the pilot; he and the editors had spent much more time than anticipated reworking the opening credits, or, as Adam called it, "tweaking the packaged open." Although I had "knocked a couple of socks off," the selection of host or hosts had not been finalized. Shooting would commence in July. It was unclear when *Viva* would start shooting; it was possible that the network would decide that I could not do both series.

Upon hanging up the telephone in my office, I walked into the dining room, where Jess was reading a manuscript.

"*Rock of Ages:* picked up for six episodes," I announced.

"Congratulations! Your own show!"

"Actually, no. It's not clear that I'm involved."

"You *are* the show."

"Okay."

"Now will you please, please get someone to negotiate this properly?"

"I will. But I'm going to wait and see if they want me. I might not be able to do both shows, and *Viva* is a better show for me."

"You can do a broader variety of things."

"Yes."

"You should be getting a payment for the show's being picked up."

"It wasn't my idea, though."

"That doesn't matter. If a movie producer has an idea and then a screenwriter writes it up, the screenwriter gets money when the project goes into production."

"But I didn't really write it, see. I was more like Talent, with a tendency to ad-lib."

"You have to stop thinking like this."

A week later Adam called back to check my availability for both shows.

Two shows!

Two days after that, he called again to say that the network wanted Emmy and me to be the cohosts of *Rock of Ages*. I whooped with joy. Mutual back-patting gave way to more practical matters.

"If I contact an agent," I said, "does he call you?"

"You can give him my name, and then I'll refer him to one of our steely negotiators."

"Okay."

"I find money discussions unpleasant."

"As do I. We must all turn our heads and look the other way."

⸻

WITH TWO SERIES in the offing, I had a certain amount of leverage with respect to finding an agent. A lot of agents, I realized, would be willing to jump on board; my impulse, however, was to reward initiative. That in mind, I decided to call Scott Arnovitz at ICM. Scott is a tall, likable fellow who represents television writers, and who, unbidden, had contacted me shortly after my first book was published, wondering if I was interested in writing for television. At the time, I was saddled with other commitments. However, he had impressed in several ways. First, he had read—or was able to create the highly convincing illusion of having read—my book. Further, he persisted in his ambitions for me, calling me again, two years later, to see if I was interested in trying to write for the *Rosie O'Donnell Show*. Since my current flare-up of activity with VH1, Jess had tendered many offers of introduction to the telemeisters at Endeavor, but this seemed perilous—I did not want the ravages of show business to seep into our relationship any more than they already had, and I wanted to be loved for *moi*.

But given the importance that Endeavor attaches to the notion of family, it might look strange if I wasn't represented by them. Particularly given that the founding partners of Endeavor had broken off from ICM. Was this my problem, though? Surely other spouses of agents had the same feelings that I did. Or was I being selfish?

I hemmed and hawed. The shores seemed rocky. Worse, the money in question was not considerable. I knew that I would be making about $2,000 an episode; so if I did six episodes of each show, I would earn about $24,000. In agent commissions, this would be 2,400 tiny American dollars—roughly, enough to buy the left lapel of an Armani suit.

I called Scott and told him about VH1, as well as that Jess was now working at Endeavor. He was interested in representing me but thought that the best course of action was to work in collaboration with an agent at Ken Lindner and Associates, an affiliate of ICM that represents on-air talent. This sounded highly auspicious to me. Moreover, the agent's name was Babette. I have always loved the name Babette. It conjures up short leather skirts and tumblers of single malt whiskey in after-hours office towers; there's a rustle of silk as she returns the dagger to its perch of black velvet.

"I have one question for you, though," Scott said.

"Why didn't I go with Endeavor?"

"Yes."

"I don't want to be the boyfriend. I would feel like anything the agency did on my behalf—or some of what they did on my behalf—was because of Jess. I'm sort of the same way with respect to *Vanity Fair.* If I sense that someone is schmoozing me because they think I'm going to write about them in *Vanity Fair,* I walk."

"You know what? I think this is all very smart. And not because I'm the beneficiary of it."

Scott, Babette, and I had a conference call the next day. Babette was on board. The operative word was *go.* I called KCRW and told Jacqueline that TV work was taking me back to New York. She congratulated me and wished me good luck. She told me to call when I got back to Los Angeles, but I knew that when I did, we would both have moved on. Reviewing theater had been wholly engrossing, not to say fascinating, and had provided an interesting filter through which to view the city. But VH1 represented an opportunity to be more overtly comedic, to enter a project from the ground floor and, in so doing, replenish the Alford coffers.

SOMETIMES LIFE THROWS pebbles on your path. Two days after Adam called to tell me that I was going to be the cohost of a television series, I—having been, for the better part of my life, dermatologically blessed—developed a largish, pimplelike excrescence on my nose. An upwelling, without surf. A volcano, without crater. Nothing approaching medical proportions, but still, highly visible and televisually distracting.

And so, having driven up to the Monterey peninsula with Jess to visit his family on the weekend, I suddenly found myself the object of intense scrutiny when Jess—sensing that a brunch at a crowded restaurant with his father, his stepmother, his sister, his niece, his brother-in-law, and his cousin was the appropriate time to discuss such matters—asked, "What's going on with your nose?"

"Just, unh . . . just some skin irritation."

"The camera is *very unkind* to that kind of thing."

Jess's dad adopted the flattened cadence of a Western porch-sitter: "Lost his job because of a boil."

⸺

BACK IN L.A., the pressure attendant to Jess's new job was rendering him manic. He would awake with a jolt at 5:00 A.M., having had only three or four hours of sleep, and wait two hours until he could start calling people in their New York offices. One morning his rustling through a stack of papers in the bedroom woke me up.

"Hi," he said. "Are you awake?"

"Not really."

"Sorry."

He then proceeded to launch into a rambling monologue—the term *spoken-word artist* comes to mind—on a host of topics: the potential blandishments of visiting our friends Richard and Caroline in London at Christmas, why I should go to El Matador beach on Saturday while he was away on a business retreat, how I should pack the cooler for a trip to El Matador, how I should take a surfing lesson with him, and how I should wait to buy a car (I was still renting) because once I started taking surfing lessons I would probably want a car that can accommodate a surfboard.

"Jesus Christ, you really know how to *ease* into a day!" I barked. "Particularly while others are still in bed."

"Gotta get to it, gotta get to it."

FOUR DAYS LATER I was back in New York, sitting in Adam's new, larger office at VH1, where we were talking about our hopes and plans for *Rock of Ages*. I felt tingly, hopeful: two television series! I was Mary *and* I was Lou Grant! I was *Touched by an Angel*, and then, while I was sitting on a rock contemplating my good fortune, a glossy mammal rubbed up against me and I realized, Hey, I've been *Touched by a Dolphin*, too! Soon I would board the speedy roadster of my future, the cathode ray as my beacon. But lingering beneath the tingle and the hope and the dolphin-touching was a vague sense of disbelief: two television series? It had happened so easily.

Indeed, this doubtfulness was not grounded in nothing. Neatly pinned to the eastern wall of Adam's office were six rows of index cards, each row composed of four cards on which were written things like "Collections" and "Aquarian"—the story ideas for *Viva*.

"It's been brought up by the powers that be that having you on both shows might overexpose you," Adam calmly told me.

"Overexpose me on VH1?"

"Yes. So think of two segments you really want to do."

A wave of disappointment and anger passed through my upper torso.

Moments later Adam was expressing concern about my "nose situation," a topic that I quickly extinguished by a vague allusion to the body's amazing ability to renew, replenish.

Moments later, Michael Rosen, a boyish, enthusiastic,

thirtysomething development person, entered, carrying a large notebook. "We've made this bible for the show," he said. "With all the segment ideas and where we want the show to go."

"And with my character arc?" I mused.

Adam speculated aloud, " 'Episode Six: Henry starts to lose interest in the show and, distracted, mistakes Michael Jackson for Prince.' "

Half an hour later, supervising producer Frank Gregory, a large, warm Brooklynite who will emerge as one of my favorite people on the shoot, ushered me to the VH1 Wardrobe Department. The two wardrobe women neatly dodged my gossip-tinged inquiries into the wardrobing proclivities of various rock stars and VH1 hosts and proffered instead an array of stylish garments bearing labels like Calvin Klein, agnes b., Katherine Hamnett, and Vestimenta. I would be dressing far beyond my means.

Encouraged to don a pair of tightish, black Armani pants and a blue-gray, large-lapeled shirt by Vestimenta, I looked in the mirror. Gone was the stoop-shouldered wearer of six-year-old Gap chinos; in his place was Hans, a foxy Danish flight attendant with a perpetual cold sore.

The following morning, walking down Bleecker Street near my apartment, I ran into a writer friend. When the conversation veered toward my burgeoning new career, she asked, "And what will you wear?"

I wondered how best to characterize the clothes; I came up with "A lot of great-looking, black, high-sheen garments."

Her eyes widened. "Are you telling me that you're going to appear on national television wearing patent leather?"

"No, I am not telling you that."

"Okay," she said. "Because that kind of thing doesn't sit so well with the editorial board of *The New York Times.*"

"No, no—not to worry," I told her. "All is tasteful, decorous."

"And flattering to your . . . shape?"

"I'm the *king* of shape."

"Okay," she relented. "You know how I worry."

ADAM CALLED ON a Wednesday to say that the network had decided I could not be on *Viva* at all. Rather than milking this opportunity for self-pity, I threw myself into *Rock of Ages* preparation. I decided that, at any given point in time, there exist four or five popular expressions that, while once funny, have, through overuse, become threadbare in their power to surprise and now serve no purpose other than to bathe their users in a pool of comedic dinge. To use them is to suggest that, from the standpoint of humor, you drive an Edsel. And so, on June 28, 1998, the eve of the first shoot of my television series—note the startling ease with which I use *my*—I found myself seated at my desk, writing down the expressions that, much in vogue, would be tempting, in the throes of filming, to fall back upon as comedic shorthand. "What's up with that?" came to mind instantly. Oft heard on MTV and VH1, this expression was being used as a postcolonic, usually preceded by the invocation of a novel or hybrid form of pop culture or consumer good; for example, "Burt Bacharach in *Austin Powers:* What's up with that?" or, in its plural form, "Mini Oreos: What's up with those?" Other trendy expressions came to mind as well, and soon they presented themselves to me as a kind of dialogue.

A: *Mini Oreos: What's up with those?*

B: *I am not gonna go there with you. No. Way. Especially right after I've just thrown up. No.*

A: *Whoa—Too Much Information. Give me the Oreos.*

B: *Would you stop eating them? We're gonna have to do an intervention on you!*

A: *Oh, don't go there. Do not go there.*
B: *You're scaring me.*
A: *You're scaring* me.

I resolved that, whenever one of these phrases popped into my head, I would try not to, ahem, go there.

CHAPTER 23

*W*E SHOT FOR THIRTEEN WEEKS. These thirteen weeks were among the most enjoyable of my professional life, the work continually evoking the yin-yang collision of opposites— it was, at once, easygoing but challenging; it was simultaneously routinized but unpredictable. I loved being a social worker of comedy, off on a home visit to determine an appropriate allocation of laughter. I loved playing car games in the van on the ride home from out-of-town shoots. I loved wearing clothing selected by a professional. I loved asking groups, any time that the singer in question was Canadian, whether the United States should annex Canada.

A system emerged. Each episode comprised four segments. Each segment required two shoots (one for each contrasting group), unless the group was a family. My participation in each shoot—most of which took place in New York City but which occasionally took us upstate or to Connecticut—averaged out to about five hours. The system was as follows: the evening before each shoot, Adam and Frank would messenger me a composite tape of the videos to be shot the next day, along with a list of questions that they wanted me to ask the group. I would watch the videos two or three times and then add my own questions to the list. Once the group was assembled on the set, I would remind them to be candid and that there were no wrong answers. We would film the group watching the videos, hoping that the images and sounds presented would induce either lip-synching or sudden emotionality. I would, prior to asking questions, turn the volume on the monitor down but keep the tape playing. After the groups had been shown the seven or eight videos, one of the cameras—either the one that had been trained on me or the one that had been on the group—would be moved back for a wide shot encompassing both me and the group, lest viewers get the impression that I had been filmed separately, in a studio just outside Tampa.

⸻

GROUP MEMBERS WERE sometimes reluctant to talk with one another or respond to one another's comments. Knowing that this was an important part of the show—"This is a discussion group, my dear! Are you the authority?" rang in my ears—I would encourage each of the groups to do it, but they didn't always heed my suggestion. Then I noticed something. One day, while the cameras were rolling, I got up from my chair and walked off camera to ask Frank something. As I did so, the group, perhaps thinking that the camera had stopped rolling, started talking to one another. This didn't really mean anything to me until one day I read, in a book about focus groups, that focus-group moderators will sometimes conduct what is called a "false closure": toward the end of the session, they will thank all the focus-group participants, thus leading the participants consciously or subconsciously to think that they are no longer being watched or recorded. But they are; and the participants' remarks during these moments often constitute their most unguarded and honest comments during the session. The practice was derived from the knowledge that, in group-therapy sessions, participants who have something awkward or painful to discuss will often wait until the last minute of the session, thus ensuring minimum airtime. I would never be so manipulative as to conduct a false closure. However, I have asked more questions of Adam and Frank during tapings than I have actually needed to have answered.

....

THE FIRST CHANGE that I experienced as a result of my foray into the televisual arts was a very noticeable one—I lost eleven pounds. If it is true, as is often said, that television puts ten pounds on you, then my eleven pounds, I realized, was, in television pounds, only one pound. However, this way of thinking did not flatter, nor did it acknowledge the hardship I had endured in order to lose the weight, so instead of thinking in terms of television pounds, I translated the whole thing into dog years. I had not lost one television pound; I had erased seventy-seven dog years.

How was I able to effect this change on my person? Two ways. First, a lot of V8. Oceans of V8; sometimes only V8 for both lunch and dinner. Second, frozen bananas. Bananas, sliced and then frozen, and thrown into a blender with a little milk and nutmeg, produce an intoxicating lo-cal treat reminiscent of fine ice cream. I call it *whippe.* Anyone who has the time and interest to go to Britain to taste the delightful concoction there that goes by the name Mr. Whippy and then, for comparison's sake, return to these shores in order to taste my own *whippe* will have firmly etched in his mind the virtues of my product: the *e* may be silent, but the superior quality is not.

I dwell here on the topic of food because, increasingly, I realized that this was my domain. On the career path on which I was currently embarked, the signposts would not read Emmy Award/small part in a Todd Solondz movie/own production company/Oscar nomination/Betty Ford, but, rather, appearance on *A Very Kenny Rogers Christmas*/Jell-O Fantasia recipe in *Redbook*/highly publicized battle with obscure form of cancer/aerobics video.

OTHER ALTERATIONS AND adjustments followed, too. The excitement and pressure of television production ratcheted up my level of zest. There was a lilt to my voice, a shuffle in my step. I was, at last, awake. Some days startlingly so: I would come home from a shoot and, pent-up, would need to throw myself into a physical activity—dancing or a long walk—to quiet the beast. I became a semifrequent presence on the dance floor of a hideous gay bar called Splash; one night I walked all the way to Brooklyn.

Two other events—possibly or possibly not related to the fact that I was feeling svelte and vibrant and necessary—occurred during the shoot. I met a zany, fun-loving group of five people at a dinner party and proceeded to convene with them seven times over the next five months. I sold two humor pieces to *The New Yorker,* a longtime dream.

In discussions about the show, Adam had, on several occasions, enlisted the word *deadpan,* and so, in my performance, I strove for a lack of affect. This seemed the right way to go, particularly as the questions that I was devising were of an absurdist bent. At our first shoot for the series—three generations of the Andersons, a black family who live outside New Haven—I asked, regarding a Lenny Kravitz video, "Is that sixties activist Angela Davis on drums?" Of a Rolling Stones video: "Is the concept here that a group of heroin addicts are having lunch in a public rest room?" And of a space-age Michael and Janet Jackson video, whether portraying Michael Jackson as a space alien was not "redundant."

The next morning, while filming a group of nine- and ten-year-old ballroom dancers (to be contrasted with senior-citizen ballroom dancers), the tall, skinny soundman walked up to me and said, "Man, you are *so dry.*"

"Yes?" I asked, trying to determine whether this was a kiss or a slap.

"Last night it was like, 'Get me a glass of water.' I was parched!"

"This isn't sounding like a compliment."

"No, it is. But I think that family was thinking, Who *is* this guy in our living room?"

I smiled at him uncertainly.

This theme—crew members needing to tell me that I was the whitest person they had ever encountered—was reasserted that afternoon when Kim, the attractive, witty makeup woman, cornered me while we were shooting record-album collectors in the East Village (to be contrasted with Sam Goody employees at the Paramus Park Mall in New Jersey).

"You remind me of a Whit Stillman character," she told me, referring to the writer/director of the haut-bourgeois comedies *Metropolitan* and *Barcelona.* "Is that your background?"

I paraphrased her question back at her: " 'Does your family have money?' "

"No, no, that's not what I mean. I mean that sort of WASPy—"

"I am a WASP. And I had an upper-middle-class, suburban upbringing."

"That's what I thought. Because, like a Whit Stillman character, you have a, unh—"

If all my acting classes had taught me anything, it was that I am able to put on my imperious high beams and, in so doing, deflect oncoming traffic. This moment with Kim seemed a particularly apt one for imperiousness; the statement "Like a Whit

Stillman character, you have a certain—" can only be followed by (*a*) "pasty, asexual quality" or (*b*) "collection of needlepoint pillows depicting dancing frogs in scuba gear."

On went the high beams.

Kim completed her statement: ". . . a confidence. You have a kind of confidence."

<hr>

I KNEW THAT, if I was going to have any success at divesting my television presence from all deadpan/just-plain-dead confusion, I would have to go to the proverbial well and find something moisture-flecked and vibrant. Ballroom had led me to Eduardo; was there a tele-equivalent? I didn't think so until one day, faced with a particularly stony group, I found myself engaging in mild flirtatiousness, feigning utter fascination with group members' every comment and trafficking in a larger-than-life ebullience that bordered on the Disneyesque. During subsequent tapings, I invoked these qualities time and time again.

Who was this man I was becoming? I did not know. However, I did know that he—part starstruck groupie, part tummler, part obsequious and slightly drunken party host—was equally appealing to both children and adults.

And that he goes by the name Mr. Buttons.

<hr>

IT WAS VERY enjoyable, on days when more than one shoot was scheduled, to kill the time between shoots by holing up in the *Rock of Ages* offices. Young production assistants, eager to curry favor, would proffer sandwiches and compliments; young producers, eager to curry favor, would proffer VH1 memorabilia and compliments. This was highly pleasurable. While I am no fan of the social phenomena peculiar to offices—the gradual massing of workers, like fish to bait, that signals that a small child is being paraded through the environs; the mass reproduction, via photocopy or E-mail, of facetiae that throws a comic light on the topic of heavy drinking or cat ownership—it was nevertheless a wonderful thing to be a visiting dignitary, to be Jack, the head of Regional Sales in the Omaha office, recently promoted to district manager, in for the week and looking for fun.

Was there ever a downside to the powerful cocktail of glamour and constant approbation? I wondered about this on the day that we were to shoot campers and their counselors at Camp Sequoia. I was picked up by a hired car in front of my building at 10:00 A.M. An hour and a half later, glancing out the car's window, I realized that I literally did not know where we were going. The makeup woman, a garment bag full of designer clothing, and I were being whisked off Somewhere, and not only did I not know the location of this Somewhere, but I had made no effort to apprehend it.

I vowed to title this episode of my life "Hairspray Ate My Brain."

MY FRIEND ALISON, a young journalist who often writes about music, knows far more about contemporary music than I do. Several times during the shoot, she took pains to limn for me the irony that, while I now had a wildly fun job in the music field, she was still doing temp work in deep Brooklyn, for an irritating man who had recently called her Sunshine.

"How's the VH1 thing going?" Alison asked me one day.

In an attempt to get up to speed with the current music scene, I had subscribed to *Rolling Stone* and *Spin* and was watching copious numbers of music videos.

"I know who Luscious Jackson is now," I told her.

"That's good," she said noncommittally.

"I am familiar with the work of both Chumbawumba and Lotion. I am prepared to discuss Hootie, Puffy, Tricky, Brandy, or Goldie."

"Well, you're . . . you're growing."

"I am."

<hr />

ALISON AND I had dinner several weeks later.

"I know who Fretblanket is," I told her somewhat defensively. She nodded in acknowledgment.

"When I need a little lift," I vamped, "I put on Sneaker Pimps, Garbage, Freak Nasty, or Rancid."

Alison smiled.

"I can tell the Black Crowes from the Counting Crows. I would never mistake the Verve for the Verve Clamp."

"Actually it's, unh, Verve *Pipe*," Alison counseled.

I glowered at her. "Don't fuck with me."

<hr />

CHIEF AMONG THE skills that the job required me to hone was an ability to project an air of unflappability. When, for instance, we were granted permission to shoot the Hell's Angels in their clubhouse in the East Village—only one other production had ever been allowed to do this—I labored long and hard not to let these gentlemen, several of whom were vividly tattooed and one of whom was named Butch, see that I was somewhat intimidated.

We showed "the brothers" (and, later, for contrast, a group of young suburban bicycle enthusiasts) videos featuring motorcycles. The brothers felt that the members of Mötley Crüe were "not tough." The brothers felt Neil Young was "a little whiny" ("Well, he's Canadian," I pointed out. "He's Canadian, but he's working in an American idiom"). I showed them the theme song for *Cops,* Inner Circle's "Bad Boys," and asked, "Do you guys think of yourselves as bad guys?"

"Sure, our public image might be, but we don't," one responded.

Butch opined, "Well, what's a bad trait? Some people think not brushing your teeth is a bad trait. Some people think a sock in the eye is a bad trait. Sometimes people *need* a sock in the eye. That doesn't mean it's a bad trait. It's just that's the way it is."

I gulped. "Unh, okay . . ."

It had occurred to me early on in the shoot that, if being on TV was to be a broadening experience, I needed to get in the habit of asking the big questions, the important questions. And so, during a somewhat sluggish discussion about the video of "Good Thing" by Fine Young Cannibals, I looked down at the monitor and beheld a strange image from that video: the camera placed on or below the floor, we are looking up between the legs of a man who, standing, is straddling his scooter. I didn't know what I wanted to say about this shot or, really, why it intrigued me, but the turban-wearing theater guru deep inside me whispered, "Darling: explore." So I plunged ahead with "When you straddle your form of transportation, are you granting the world permission to concentrate on"—here I took my right index finger and drew a large, slow-motion circle around my groin area—"*this area?*"

The brothers shifted uncomfortably in their seats; the one with the long, dirty-blond hair said, "I don't know where you're going with this line of questioning."

"Well, I just wondered if, when you ride a Harley, if you, unh, er . . ."

Fumble, fumble.

I moved on. A video by a group called Big Ass Truck set off

much conversation. I asked, "Now, am I right in thinking that if you have a nice-looking Harley, you refer to it as a *boss hog*?"

The brothers all laughed at me, and one volunteered, "That might be the yuppie term. That's the first time I've heard that one."

Shortly thereafter, one brother's statement that certain styles of motorcycles are more cool than others made me wonder if Angels ever had a "day" bike and a "night" bike; this question drew slightly hostile stares. I asked what the Angels would do if—as happens in the Big Ass Truck video—someone knocked their bikes over: "Would you get pig-biting mad?"

Stares, stares, stares. Finally, one Angel: "I wouldn't be happy."

Just then, one of the cameramen announced that he needed to reload tape. During the brief break, Kim, the makeup woman, materialized in front of me, bearing powder.

" 'Pig-biting mad'?" she whispered, daubing my nose. "Were you looking for a fight?"

"No. Nor was I when I asked if they had a day bike and a night bike. In fact, I held back that time. I was going to ask if there was the motorcycle equivalent of 'the little black dress.' "

Kim asked what I meant.

"You know," I explained, "a motorcycle that would take you from day *into* evening."

I could read Kim's expression. Kim's expression read, "You and I will be walking out of the clubhouse separately."

DID EMMY AND I have long, boozy lunches whereat we swapped cohostly tidbits like who was the cutest gaffer, or how best to subtly elongate our questions and responses during taping so as to achieve maximum "face time"? No. Conversely, did we slink past each other in the hallways of Wardrobe, teetering on the brink of catfight? No. In fact, since we shot our segments separately, I did not see her for the entirety of the shoot. In the middle of the shoot, Frank called me one night and said, "Just so you know, Emmy won't be at the press shoot tomorrow."

"Is she okay?"

"Something's come up."

"She doesn't want to be on the show anymore?"

"She got a movie role."

Emmy had been cast as the best friend in *Superstar,* the movie based on Molly Shannon's *Saturday Night Live* character Mary Katherine Gallagher. At the conclusion of the six-episode cycle, she would be leaving the show.

During the photo shoot the next day, I felt lonely. I wanted banter, frivolity, lattes. What might have seemed enviable— being the sole object of the photographer's attention—felt diminishing rather than elevating. I felt like I was walking down the cordoned-off entrance to the Oscars without a date. On the upside, however, Emmy's departure meant that I would get to do more segments than originally promised. This augured well.

———

THE MORE GROUPS I interviewed, the more I noticed that I tend to get as good as I give. Which is to say that if, as interviewer, you open up or make people laugh or break down some barrier, your interviewees are more likely to follow suit. The days on which I was willing to act as if I were metaphorically pantsless were often the days that we got the best comments from the groups. And so, in an attempt to spur an opinion from group members, I have feigned ignorance of a large number of topics, performed a small Irish jig, laughed harder than was warranted, purposefully fumbled comments and then resaid them so as to keep group members from becoming uncomfortable when we asked them to repeat their comments, and indulged an eighty-year-old in her belief that at least two music videos of the late 1980s feature performances by George Washington. Are such actions manipulative? No. They are the grease in the proverbial skillet. An ounce of artifice can enliven a pound of reality.

I MISSED JESS. This was the longest we had ever been separated. However, during the six weeks that we didn't see each other, I started to think about him with a reverence and ardor that I never had before. It suddenly made sense to me why almost all of the actors I am friends with are married and were married at a young age: given the vagaries of show business, marriage is an anchor. You may have a job tomorrow or you may not, but at least you know you're still hitched.

One day, after a seven-hour shoot out on Long Island with the suburban bike kids had ended at nine-thirty and had been followed the next morning by a seven o'clock shoot with young brides-to-be, I needed a delightful treat, so I bought myself breakfast at Elephant & Castle, a restaurant in my neighborhood. Hunkered down in the warm embrace of my table in the far corner of the restaurant, I found myself conducting an imaginary conversation with Jess. We had been to this restaurant together many times before, and somehow this made it even easier to see him sitting across from me. As our imagined dialogue started unspooling itself from my brain, I nodded my head at one of his "responses," and then, unbidden, spoke aloud, "I *know*."

Had my feelings of separation metamorphosed into mental illness?

THE SHOW DEBUTED on Tuesday, August 25, at 9:00 P.M. and then re-aired, as it would during the course of its run, three scheduled times during the week. The reviews, though limited in number, were highly favorable in tone. None described me as human Brie. Rather, I elicited one rose and one tomato: the New York *Daily News* gushed that I was "an absolute master of deadpan, schoolmarmish questioning," but the *Chicago Tribune* carped, "It's unfortunate that one of the *Rock of Ages* interviewers frequently insinuates himself into the conversation rather than let people's thoughts shine through. Laybourne, who has performed stand-up comedy, is fairly straightforward when soliciting remarks from the Mets and Little Leaguers in separate locations. But Alford, labeled a humorist . . . acts as if he wants to follow in Laybourne's comedy footsteps. Apparently the Chuckle Shack wasn't open when he needed to get stand-up aspirations out of his system."

I vowed never to utter the words *deep dish* again.

While the ratings during the re-airings would go up, the debut was not spectacular. Tuesday night at nine, it turned out, was a tough nut, ratings-wise: not only would we be up against *Frasier* and *Spin City* once the fall season started, but even before that we had to contend with one of the summer's two breakout hits—Fox's *Guinness World Records: Prime Time*. During our debut episode, a man on *Guinness World Records* removed his prosthetic nose: ratings heaven. Twelve million viewers tuned in, rapt and appalled, wallowing in the you-are-there splendor of nasal displacement. Each week I would read the show's description in *TV Guide* (Week One: "spitting crickets for distance," Week Two: "A woman who eats broken glass," Week Three: "A man sits in a tub of rattlesnakes," and so on, until, a few weeks after we were off the air, "A man squirts milk from his eye in an attempt to establish a distance record").

I cringed on two levels.

⸻

AS THE EPISODES aired, I received tens of enthusiastic phone calls from friends and family and several slightly less enthusiastic calls from people I'd been in acting classes with. A spiffy commercial for the show, featuring clips from various episodes, including one in which I ask, about the macarena, "Is there an element of . . . butt-wiggling?" had been put together; VH1, wonderfully, seemed to be running it upward of five times a day (in addition to the four scheduled weekly showings of each episode, VH1 was also occasionally airing the episodes on an unscheduled basis). I twice had the strange sensation, during the run of the first six episodes, of turning my TV on in the middle of the commercial. Being on TV so much felt not unlike having a Cyborg clone of myself. If I wasn't watching an episode when it was airing, if I didn't keep a nervous eye on the clone, what might he get up to? I worried that he might grow a brain.

But the steady trickle of compliments was like catnip. Granted, not all of the compliments were wholly positive; the commercial and print ads for the show included the tag line "Everyone's a critic" and, in so doing, seemed to beg for candor. My friend Francine left a message on my machine that included the statement "I felt a little shy when you said *jigginess* on national television"; an acquaintance reported to me that I looked like I was "really trying hard."

I was recognized by a stranger only once during this first batch of shows. An employee at Coconuts music store on Sixth Avenue walked up to me once and said, "You know who you look like, or might even be?"

"Who?" I asked.

"Rock of Ages."

It was only my sense of decorum that kept me from informing this young man that he had just met Morley Safer and referred to him as *60 Minutes.*

The strangest comment came from my friend Lynn. She had mentioned the show to a friend of hers, who said he had seen it and who then referred to it as "the show with the psychiatrist."

"He's not a psychiatrist," Lynn said. "He's a writer. I know him."

"Oh, I'm not thinking of the same show, then."

"No, you are," Lynn told him. "But he's not a psychiatrist."

"He's not?"

No. But I am no stranger to the term *borderline.*

MY BRUSH WITH fame and its attendant power to swell the ego led me, one Monday, to do something I had not foreseen— I committed a suspect charitable action. Feeling that the tenor of my professional life had taken on a particularly chipper and Cole Porter–like flavor—there would be no more bluuuuuue songs, only hoop-de-hooooo songs—I had gone for a walk. At a construction site in Chelsea I saw a tough-looking kid about twelve years old using a squeegee and a bucket to post bills on a wooden barricade. It looked like it was a bigger job than he could handle.

"Here, let me help you," I said, holding a poster in place for him. I felt slightly virtuous.

"That's alright," he said, clearly irritated.

"It's no problem," I said.

"Listen, I'm working alone," he said, turning his back to me.

Looking back on the incident now, what intrigues me about it is that my reaction at the time had been not to apologize to the kid for the embarrassment I might have caused him but rather something more self-centered: I turned around, looking at the nearby intersection, hoping that someone I knew had seen me helping the kid out.

The *New York Post* once reported that Eddie Murphy had been seen tossing money into the streets of Harlem from a moving limo; Jim Carrey has said, "The most enjoyable things I've ever given to anybody in my life were when I used to go around writing 'Have a good day' on twenty-dollar bills or five-dollar bills and leaving them in places where people would find them, on park benches, or where I know there's a lot of foot traffic. I'd stick it in the sidewalk, then I would go away." While Murphy's and Carrey's charity stems from a different set of circumstances from mine, our three approaches are linked: they are all essentially narcissistic and help to create a definition of charity wherein the doing of the charitable act is more important than the charitable act itself. After all, if you truly want to help someone, you find a needy person or cause and then determine that person or cause's needs. But to distribute your largesse without an assessment of need, as I had—you might as well, unh, throw your money in the street.

CHAPTER 24

I FLEW BACK TO Los Angeles for a long weekend. Our apartment felt slightly alien to me. Upon entering it, I had the distinct impression of spending the weekend at my divorced dad's apartment—I pawed through a stack of magazines to see what the current subscriptions were; I noticed that two pieces of decorative crockery, formerly ensconced in the kitchen, were now in the dining room.

One night, as we were walking out of Jess's office at Endeavor, he looked down the long row of desks belonging to the agents' assistants and, with nary a shred of irony, said to me, "I love those kids."

I rolled my eyes heavenward. *Kids?*

"What?" Jess asked.

"O to have a small air-sickness bag."

"But I do. I really do."

" 'Ladies and gentlemen: my very, *very* special friend, Jess Taylor.' "

On Saturday night Jess had to go to a charity benefit honoring one of the Endeavor clients. He had invited me but in such a way as to make clear that, were I to come, I would occupy a place in his devotions somewhere near that of the parking valet. Saturday morning he told me, "I'm going to borrow your blue shirt to wear to the dinner tonight."

"Oh, I'll just stay in and have a cup of bouillon."

"Listen, if I had spent the summer avoiding my boyfriend just to be on basic cable, I don't think I'd be casting aspersions."

"I SWEAR TO God—you put a wedding ring on a man and he turns into a large, neutered animal!"

It was a Sunday morning, and Jess, on the phone since four A.M., was trying to badger the recently married Charles into going with him to the Farmers Market to eat donuts. But Charles wanted to stay home with Sandra.

Then Jess turned his beacon of expectation on me: *I* will go to the Farmers Market with him to eat donuts. He entered my office and started pacing, pacing.

"I don't think so. But thanks," I said, engrossed in the article I was writing. "I'm having a series of small, internal, literary moments."

"Emphasis on the small."

"Jess, honey, you need to redirect that energy," I said, suddenly Stella Adler. "It's wonderful energy—*it will find a home*—but it needs a better target."

"Donuts calling!"

While I was enthused to see that Jess's vocational pursuits had energized, not to say transformed, him into a powerhouse of nuclear fission, it sometimes felt precarious to be living downstream from the plant. Hair might be singed.

WHEN I LEARNED that the network had renewed *Rock of Ages* for another eight episodes, I experienced jubilation and relief: the baby lives, the baby walks. Back in New York, Adam, Frank, and Michael Rosen took me out for a celebratory dinner at a posh Italian restaurant, where I ordered a large piece of meat.

For the second cycle of *Rock of Ages,* I tried to increase my stake in the show. I made a list of segment ideas, several of which, with tinkering, were approved by the powers that be. I proposed names of possible new cohosts. I badgered my colleagues in postproduction to include my favorite moments from the shoots. And, most important: I have asked all my friends, whenever introducing me to their friends or colleagues, to always refer to me as "television's Henry Alford."

A highly favorable review of the show, and of *Rock Candy,* ran in *Time* the week our new season was launched—"rock comedy hasn't been this smart since *This Is Spiñal Tap.*" The review also stated, "Cheery co-host Henry Alford elicits lines from small children that Bill Cosby sweats whirlpools trying to score."

Calgonite, take me away.

CHAPTER 25

EGRETS, I HAVE A FEW. How did I miss the bus headed to Interesting Character Actor Who Appears Only in Dangerous, Edgy Independent Films and end up instead on Person Who Helps Others Make Jokes About Lycra on Cable Television? Why is my head shot, splattered with marinara sauce, not the prize possession of every restaurant owner in New York City? Why have I never put together an evening of ballroom entitled "Eduardo: Elusive Muse"? Why have I never secured a berth on the rickety ocean liner of improv comedy? Why has a heavyset talent agent named Myrna, calling to explain that we are going to renegotiate the contract for my Broadway hit, never trilled over my phone, "We're going to reno, dollface. We're going to reno"?

It is madness to dwell on what I am not. Moreover, looked at in a certain light—a highly self-serving light—being a television personality is more creative than traditional acting. The television personality, after all, cannot hide behind interpretation or textual analysis—he is not doing a Danny Zuko or a Lady Capulet like we have never seen Danny Zuko or Lady Capulet done before—because he can only offer himself. He is the character, the character is him. Complaints about his performance should be addressed to:

MY EGO
1374 MY PERSONALITY WAY
MY LIMITATIONS AS A HUMAN, MY LIFE
02179

Thank you.

....

WHAT WILL BE *Rock of Ages*'s legacy? I do not know. Will the focus group become a new entertainment genre? Will the show be canceled before you read this? Will one of the segments spin off into its own show like *Rock of Ages* itself did? Will random groups of people, separated by age, profession, or interest, start to meet on the street to mouth off on a variety of issues, interspersing their comments to comic effect?

Some things we can never know. Indeed, if there is a lesson that emerges from my time in the glamour trenches, it is that you can never be certain. What might be, might be; but then again, it might not. Therefore, have contingencies. Be prepared, as the adage runs, to improvise.

Have I found my niche? That is a big word for my modest skills and even more modest advances. I am reminded at this point of Mrs. John Gotti. I once read an interview with Mrs. Gotti in which, asked if she knew what her husband does for a living, she remarked, "All I know is, he provides." That's not unlike how I feel with respect to my foray into the performing arts. While a part of me longs to pinpoint the precise fluctuations in my spirit that have arisen as a result of standing in front of various groups of people and screaming, "Look at me, look at me!" another part of me knows that there is no mathematics for such things. All I know is, it provides.

CHAPTER 26

I TALK TO MORE strangers on airplanes now than I have at any other time in my life. One of the people I befriended on a plane was a small, hearty psychotherapist from Denver. I liked her immediately, and she made me laugh when she said that she, too, felt like she was living in two cities—I asked, "Denver and . . . ," and she promptly replied, "New York/La Guardia."

She asked a lot of questions about Jess and me—why we hadn't moved in together when we lived in New York, if it was difficult to be away from him when I was in New York. I had also told her about some of my writing, as well as about my performing, and as she asked questions about my work, it was clear that she was trying to put me in the provocateur/firebrand category, a category I don't aspire to.

At one point in the conversation I found myself saying, "I think doing comedy improv for a paying audience was the scariest. That, or maybe the Meisner basement."

"For a lot of creative people like yourself the biggest scare is realizing that you're not just an artist."

I wasn't sure what she meant. I asked, "You mean, the scariest thing for me is to accept that I'm normal?"

She grinned and said, "You seem a little hostile to the idea."

"No, I'm not. Or I am. I don't know. It's just that the idea is . . ."

"What?"

"Well, if you'll excuse me, it's a little trite."

She lifted her eyebrows, the facial equivalent of a shoulder shrug.

I thought about her idea more. "But I guess it's true," I said. "I guess it's true. It's trite, but it's true."

"Most of life's lessons are. They just seem more interesting and unusual when you're caught up in the middle of them."

JESS AND I are lying on the couch. Moments ago, Jess was roaming around the kitchen, where he spilled a glass of seltzer, breaking the glass and causing him to curse; I have encouraged him to come into the living room and relax. I have propped pillows behind my back; Jess is lying partially on top of me, his head resting on my chest. I am reading a novel aloud to him. I am holding said novel high up in the air with my right hand, and I am clutching it firmly lest it suddenly plummet onto our heads and set in motion a chain of events requiring reconstructive surgery.

Over the course of the twenty minutes or so that I have been reading, I have noticed that Jess's heartbeat, semihammering at first, has now slowed to a steady lub-*dub*. Then, three pages later, Jess's lack of response to a clever rejoinder made by the novel's protagonist makes me realize that he has fallen asleep.

I think, Good. I think, My work here is done. I think, Niche City.

I put the book down on the coffee table. I fall asleep, too.

Epilogue

"WHAT'S THAT?" a friend visiting from out of town asked one Thursday as we were crossing Sheridan Square, just two blocks away from Jess's and my New York apartment, on our way to a party in the East Village. She was referring to a crowd of people letting loose a volley of bickering and caterwauling as they made their way past the Citibank on Christopher Street. I explained that she was looking at the cast and audience of *Tony and Tina's Wedding,* the interactive, site-specific show in which audience members become the guests at an Italian-American wedding.

"Oh, right," my friend said, registering this vaguely. "Have you seen it?"

"Seen it?" I asked. "I'm in it."

Indeed, although the producers and cast of the show are unaware of it, for several years now I have been playing a small role in the show. You might recognize me: I play Guy at ATM Machine?

Actually, I started out as Person Exiting Subway Stop, but over time, my role has changed—I'm always *finding* things— and I have also been Churlish Passerby, Pizza Enthusiast, New Garment Owner, Actor Carrying Manila Envelope Full of Head

Shots, Guy Trying to Whistle Difficult Randy Newman Composition, Pajama Guy, Furtive Glancer, Stoner, and, one evening two summers ago, Inebriant #7. Even when the show moved its base of operations up to the theater district last year, I continued to give the show my all: I'm a survivor.

It's *nothing*, really, Guy at ATM Machine—it's just a tiny moment, all I do is walk into the Citibank, insert my card into the machine, and leave: nothing, I'm filler, really. I mean, I could practically be a cardboard cutout for all the audience notices me. You could remove me and virtually no one would be the wiser; I'm just a tiny azalea bush on the theatrical landscape—a tiny, dust-covered azalea bush on the theatrical landscape. It's just me, doing what I do every day, not a big deal. If my part were any smaller I'd be crew, *cameo* is too big a word; think Cecil B. DeMille and then multiply by 5,000. I swear, it's gotten totally blown out of proportion, if the other cast members had any idea that I'd been nattering on this long about my walk-on, they'd be amazed, they'd think I was trying to horn in on their hard-won turf, like I was some kind of egomaniacal Stage Door Johnny trying to hitch his proverbial wagon, but I swear to you I would never stoop so low—I mean, I *wish* I could be that ambitious—but you have to remember this is just one of the things I do, I'm a writer, really—humor for magazines—but it's fun to flex different muscles, fun not to have to be the star *all* the time—surely there are more interesting things we could talk about besides my career? Because, after all, I'm not really an actor, at least not in the sense of "Oh, he's an actor," which is to say, I'm *very, very self-effacing,* I could never be as self-absorbed as actors have to be, the way they talk and talk about themselves, because really all I'm trying to do is make other people look good. I'm trying to create an atmosphere in which they can do their best work; I'm just a catalyst, I'm trying to keep all the character work and all the choices buried underneath so that I seem completely organic to the situation. I'm just a booster shot of *tone,* that's all. I'm a vacuum, I'm a mirror, I'm absence, I'm Heisenberg himself. If I were a state? Delaware.

So that's probably why you didn't recognize me when you picked up this book.

I thought *you* looked familiar, actually.

Wait a minute—you're not Person on Street Corner, are you?

Oh, my God—it's you!

We meet at last.

ACKNOWLEDGMENTS

THE AUTHOR WISHES TO EFFUSE OVER HIS EDITOR,
THE WONDERFUL JON KARP,
AS WELL AS LAURA BLAKE PETERSON,
BETH PEARSON, MARGARET WIMBERGER,
DANIEL REMBERT, PENELOPE GREEN,
BRIAN MCLENDON, MICHAEL SOLOMON,
SAM SIFTON, DAVID HANDELMAN, DIANA FROST,
AMY ASTLEY, HALLIE SPORN,
LAUREN ZALAZNICK, RAELLE KOOTA, AND
THE FOLKS AT BROADWAY, ANN CAMPBELL,
AMANDA GROSS, AND RODRIGO CORRAL.